"You will be home before the leaves have fallen from the trees."

Kaiser Wilhelm II
to German soldiers, August 1914

The war to end all wars

WORLD WAR ONE

1914-1918

CAMPFIRE®

KALYANI NAVYUG MEDIA PVT LTD

The war to end all wars
WORLD WAR ONE
1914-1918

Written by:	Alan Cowsill
Illustrated by:	Lalit Kumar Sharma
Inking by:	Jagdish Kumar
Colorists:	Pradeep Sherawat, Vijay Sharma
Editors:	Jason Quinn, Aadithyan Mohan
Lettering:	Bhavnath Chaudhary
Design:	Era Chawla
Cover Art:	Lalit Kumar Sharma, Jagdish Kumar, Vijay Sharma

CAMPFIRE®

www.campfire.co.in

Mission Statement

To entertain and educate young minds by creating unique illustrated books
that recount stories of human values, arouse curiosity in the world around us,
and inspire with tales of great deeds of unforgettable people.

Published by Kalyani Navyug Media Pvt Ltd
101 C, Shiv House, Hari Nagar Ashram,
New Delhi 110014, India

ISBN: 978-93-80741-85-7

Printed in India

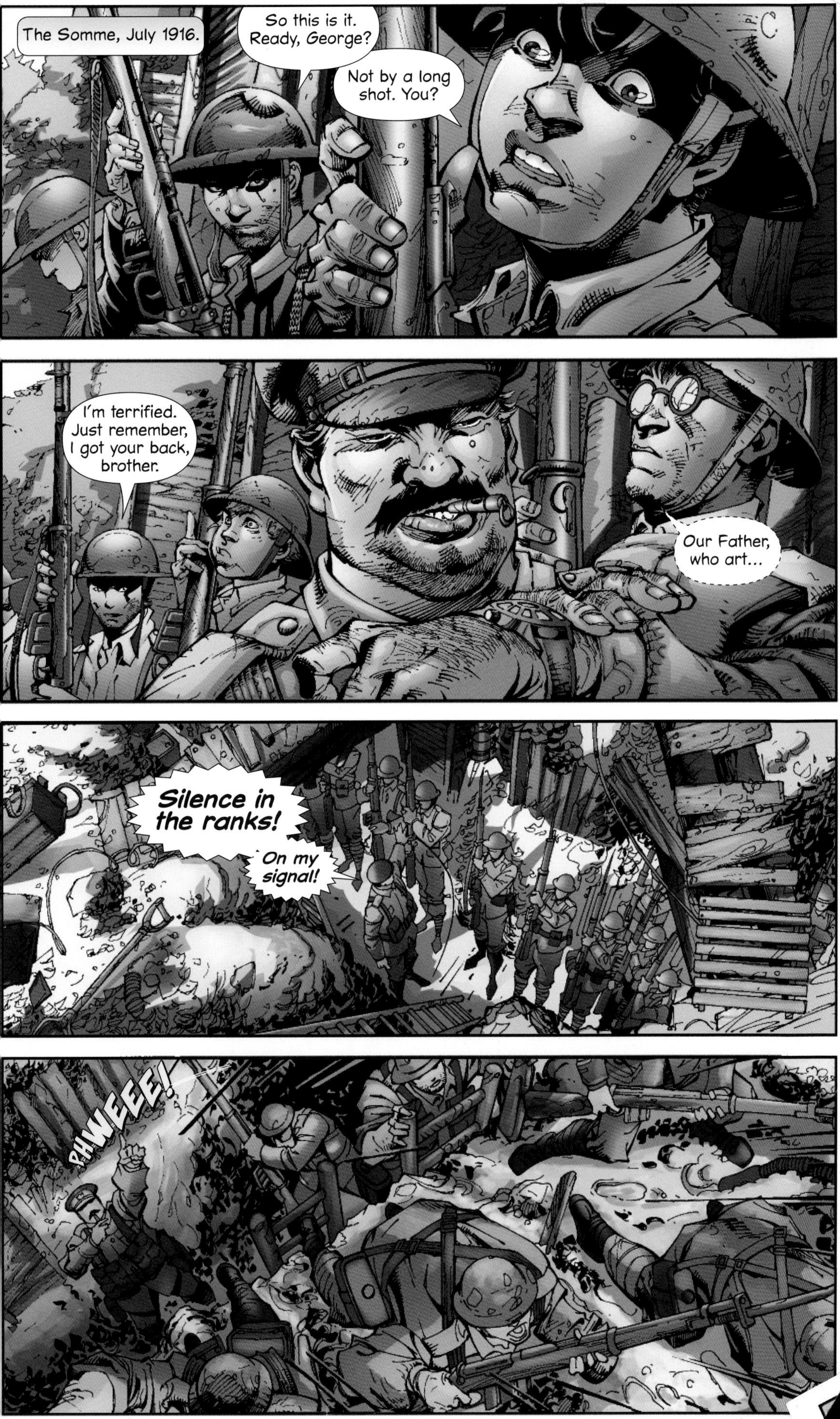
The Somme, July 1916.
So this is it. Ready, George?
Not by a long shot. You?
I'm terrified. Just remember, I got your back, brother.
Our Father, who art...
Silence in the ranks!
On my signal!
PHWEEE!

It was supposed to be over by Christmas. The war to end all wars. In the end it lasted four long years...

...and killed over 16 million people, injuring 20 million more.

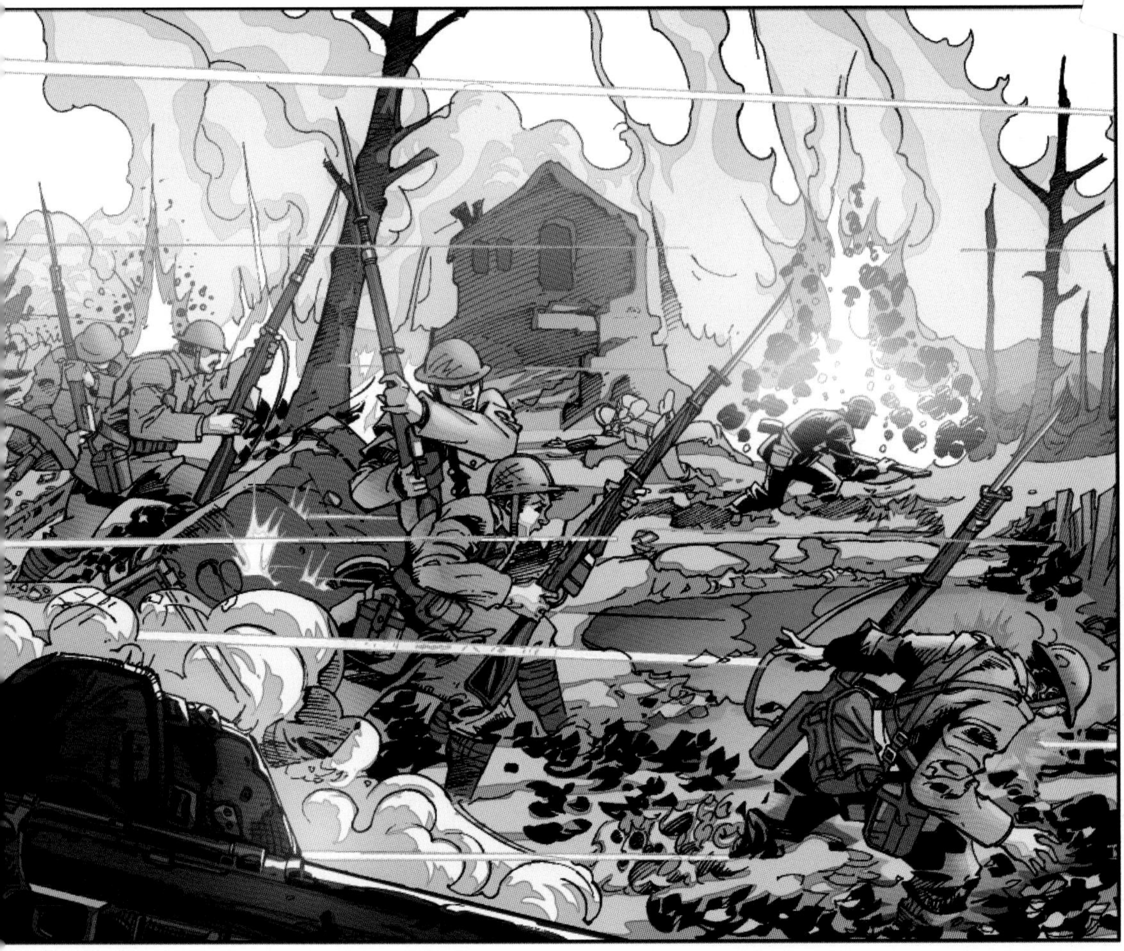

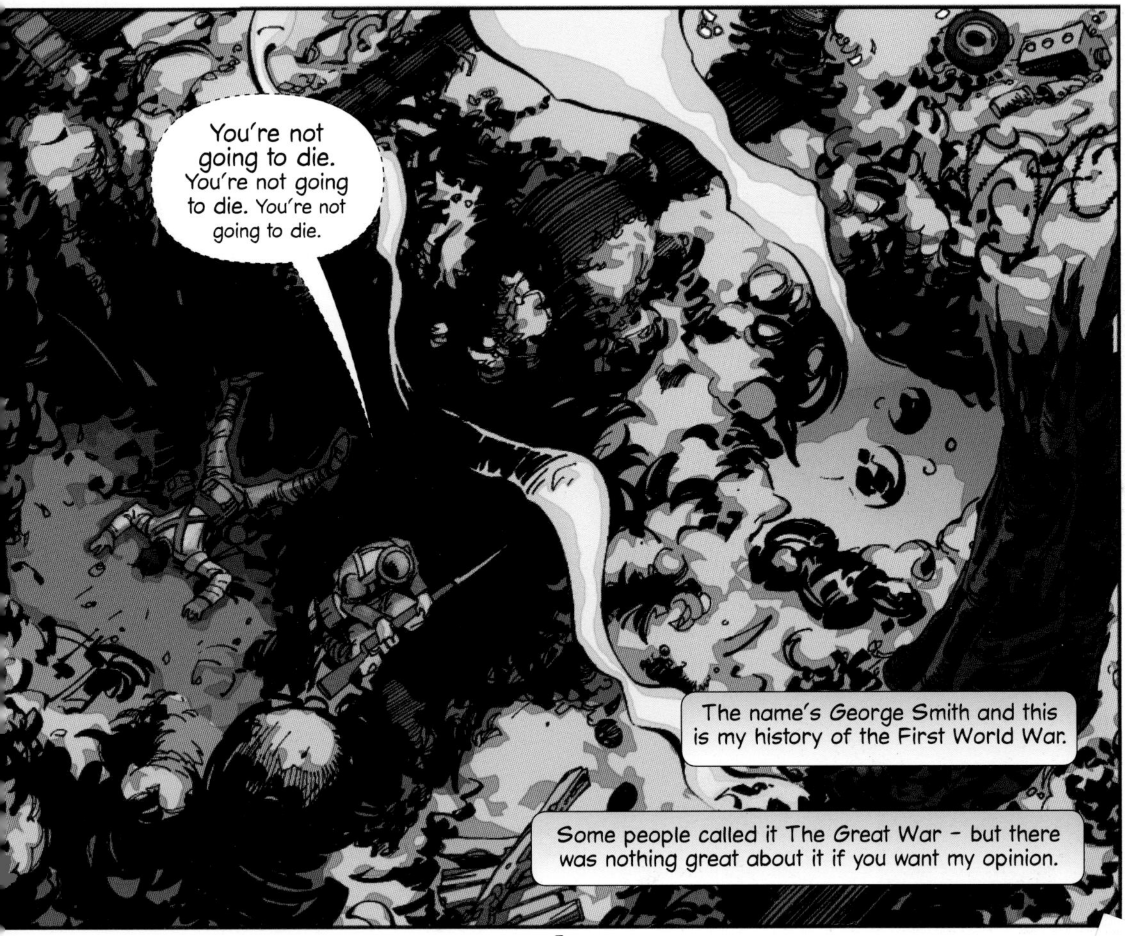
You're not going to die. You're not going to die. You're not going to die.
The name's George Smith and this is my history of the First World War.
Some people called it The Great War - but there was nothing great about it if you want my opinion.

It might have been the Twentieth Century but many of our leaders still acted like it was the Nineteenth...

Kaiser Wilhelm II of Germany was taking an aggressive stance as the country began to rival Britain as a major economic power.

That was a factor that drove Britain closer to the French. The two nations signed the *Entente Cordiale* in 1904. The French and Russians were also allies, which left the Germans worried that they were surrounded on all sides by potential enemies.

Germany formed an alliance with Austria-Hungary, Bulgaria and the Ottoman Empire, collectively they were known as the *Central Powers.*

Advances in science and industry were taking the production of armaments to undreamed of levels.

The Industrial Revolution was about to change the face of war forever.

There hadn't been a full-scale European war for nearly a hundred years. Some fools even started to think a war would be a good thing. By 1914, Europe was a powder keg waiting to explode. All it needed was a spark... or a bullet.

UNITED KINGDOM

GERMANY

RUSSIA

FRANCE

AUSTRIA-HUNGARY

PORTUGAL

SPAIN

SERBIA

BULGARIA

BlackSea

GREECE

TURKEY

The bullet – or two bullets to be precise – came from the gun of Gavrilo Princip.

NAME – GAVRILO PRINCIP
BORN – 25 JULY 1894
ETHNICITY – SERB

Princip was a member of the Black Hand; a secret Serbian nationalist organization, secretly led by Dragutin Dimitrijevic, the Head of Serbian Intelligence.

Dimitrijevic wanted to build a Greater Serbia which would include Bosnia, at the time part of the Austro-Hungarian Empire.

The arms have been smuggled into Sarajevo but I'm not sure how reliable these people are.

If they can assassinate Archduke Ferdinand, it will be a great moment for our cause and if not, a little chaos won't hurt us.

"Either way, I doubt history will remember a few dying students."

›kof.. kof..‹

Trifko Grabez

Vaso Cubrilovic

Cvjetko Popovic

Mehmed Mehmedbasic

Nedeljko Cabrinovic

Danilo Ilic

Gavrilo Princip had tuberculosis. He was dying but filled with nationalistic fervor...

...the two made a deadly combination.

It's almost time. Today we strike a blow for freedom.

Little is known about their roles. Some suggest Princip was the leader, others Ilic.

Cabrinovic, you will use the bomb. The seven of us will spread out along the route on Appel Quay.

If any of you fail, take the cyanide. We can't afford to be caught until the deed is done.

On the morning of June 28th, 1914, Cabrinovic took up his position, mingling in with the crowds that had come to see the heir to the throne of the Austro-Hungarian Empire.

Look! There they are!

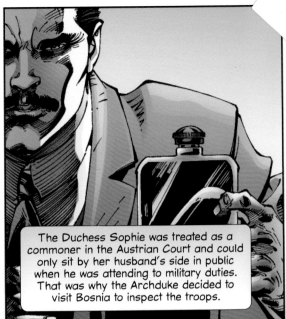

The Duchess Sophie was treated as a commoner in the Austrian Court and could only sit by her husband's side in public when he was attending to military duties. That was why the Archduke decided to visit Bosnia to inspect the troops.

After inspecting the army, the royal couple visited Sarajevo, to open the new state museum.

KLANG

It should have been a happy occasion...

For a greater Serbia!

Cabrinovic made one basic error. The bomb took ten seconds to detonate after it had been primed.

Sophie, get down!

It bounced off the Archduke's car and destroyed the car behind them.

BOOM!

What are you waiting for? Drive, you idiot!

The would-be assassin tried to drown himself in the river, but sadly for him, the water only came up to his ankles...

Come here, you!

They've arrested Cabrinovic.

They must know about us now. He'll talk. They'll make him talk.

I've heard the Archduke is carrying on as normal. He's meeting the Mayor right now.

Just keep calm, and don't panic.

Maybe we'll get a second chance.

I wonder what was going through Princip's head that morning. No one knows what exactly brought him down Franz Joseph Street.

Have you heard? Someone tried to kill the Archduke. His friend's in hospital. Who would do such a thing?

Some even say he bought a sandwich at Moritz Schillers' Deli.

It was the worst kind of luck for Ferdinand. He was going to visit the injured in hospital when his car turned into Franz Joseph Street.

What are you doing? This is the wrong way!

The Archduke... I don't believe it!

Not only did they take the wrong turn but the car stalled – right in front of Princip.

Princip had been expelled from school for taking part in demonstrations against the Austro-Hungarian authorities. Ever since, he had been trying to make a name for himself amongst the various anti-Austrian factions.

Fate offered him the perfect opportunity.

And the rest...

...as they say...

RIAM BLAM

...is history.

"I have struck a blow for freedom. Those shots will be heard around the world."

Anti-Serbian riots broke out in Sarajevo. Austria-Hungary was out for blood. The Germans gave them a 'blank check', promising to back whatever they did in response.

Austria-Hungary wanted a war with Serbia. They sent the country a list of demands and when Serbia accepted all but one of them, used it as a pretext to attack.

Russia came to Serbia's aid as the fires of war started to spread. France backed Russia and when the Germans marched through Belgium to attack France on August 4th, Britain declared war on Germany.

Many cheered when war was declared but some, like the British Foreign Secretary Edward Grey, saw the danger...

The lamps are going out all over Europe. We shall not see them lit again in our lifetime.

Within just six weeks of Archduke Ferdinand's assassination, the world was at war.

Britain came aflame with anti-German sentiment almost as soon as war was declared.

Can't believe they've invaded Belgium. What's Belgium ever done to anyone?

You don't even know where Belgium is.

What is Belgium, anyway?

What's that noise – sounds like trouble?

CRASH!

The whole town's gone crazy!

They're smashing Hanz' barber shop up. Why?

Smash it up before he can slit our throats!

He's a German... guess we're at war with him too.

But I only met him yesterday. He was showing me his new dog.

BARBER

Get the dog. It's trying to escape!

Come here boy!

Oi! Why are you protecting that dog? Don't you know it's German?

It's just a puppy and it's done nothing wrong.

You got a problem with my kid brother, Dennis?

Sorry, Joe. Didn't know he was your brother. All's good. Just a misunderstanding that's all.

Maybe you're some kind of Jerry sympathizer. Maybe you need a lesson.

You're back.

Only for the night. Shipping out tomorrow.

Must be exciting, going to war.

Hopefully it won't last long. Some say it'll be over by Christmas.

Bet I don't even see any action.

Joe was mistaken. He was soon in the thick of it. He was part of the British Expeditionary Force (BEF) that disembarked in France on August 7th, 1914.

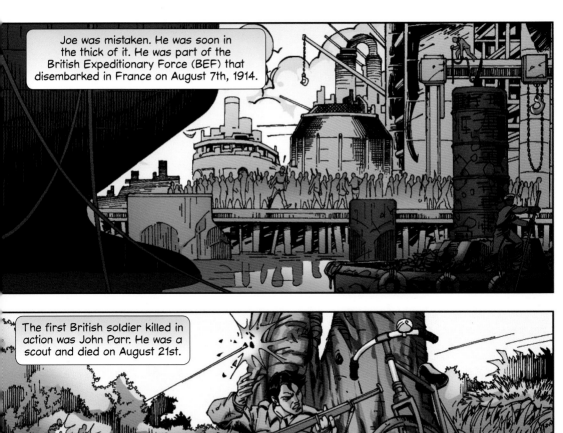

The first British soldier killed in action was John Parr. He was a scout and died on August 21st.

Parr was killed near Mons, where Joe and the BEF had their first real confrontation with the enemy.

The Royal Flying Corps had only been formed in 1912. At the start of the war, the pilots were mostly used for reconnaissance missions.

Better get back to base. Looks like the Germans are closer than we thought.

Sir, I've spotted the enemy near Waterloo. The area's crawling with German soldiers.

What's that?

Oh, you're a pilot. Must be terribly cold up there in your plane.

Sorry, sir?

Must be a dashed dangerous business too. Whatever would you do if your engine packed in?

Well, you just hope for the best, sir.

Now, about these numbers. I wrote them down. The fields are alive with the enemy.

Yes, I'm sure you thought you saw the enemy but our information proves you simply couldn't have. Dismissed.

Can't believe that fella. Do yourself a favor, son, make sure you have your rifle ready for action...

You're going to have some uninvited guests real soon.

The pilot was right. Joe and his pals had only just finished their trench when an explosion rattled them.

BOOM!

What the...

It was August 23rd, 1914. The Battle of Mons had started, the BEF's first serious contact with the enemy.

Wait for it... wait...

Fire!

The British held their own on the first day but were hopelessly outnumbered. 70,000 against a German force of 160,000.

By the end of the first day, the order was given to retreat.

Been walking for days, don't think I can feel my feet...

Count yourself lucky. Mine have been bleeding for the last two days.

By the time the news of Mons reached us, I was already feeling the need to help. Call it patriotism if you will. An old fashioned concept but at the time it meant a lot to me — and my mate Fred.

Come on, let's join. You're always saying you want more adventure.

It's not about the adventure. I just want to do my bit.

And it'll be more fun than working on the farm.

BRITONS

"YOU" JOIN YOUR COUNTRY'S ARMY

GOD SAVE THE KING

Welcome lads. Good to see you're all willing to do your duty for King and country.

How old are you, boy?

Sixteen, sir.

You do realize that you need to be eighteen to join the army?

Oh, sorry sir. I'm eighteen I am. Honest.

Excellent. I do like a man of his word. Welcome to the army, lads. Next stop France!

He was wrong about that. The next stop was basic training – but only after everyone gave us a smashing send off!

My mum cried when I told her but the family still came out to watch me leave.

I think the whole town's here!

Hey, George, there's your Martha.

I'd started walking out with Martha a few weeks before. I was going to miss her more than anyone...

Take this photo. Had it done special like, so you won't forget me.

There's no way anyone could ever forget you, Martha.

Be safe, George. Please be safe.

Come on, George, hurry up or you'll miss the war!

It was a great photo and I didn't forget Martha. There were times when the thought of her was the only good thing in my life.

That photo became my most treasured possession. I still have it. One day I'll give it to the grandkids.

I'm not sure what we expected when we got to the camp but what we found took us all by surprise.

Guess this is about as basic as training gets.

Wonder where we can get a cup of tea?

The first few weeks was made up of basic training. There wasn't enough accommodation for us all so we ended up camping on a common. It was fine at first but miserable in winter.

The other right, Smith!

Well done, Smith. We'll make a soldier out of you yet!

The basic training lasted for 12 weeks and even then we didn't go to war. Then it was time to move to our battalions, where the real training started.

While we were stuck training, the war was spreading out across the whole world.

GERMANY

BELGIUM

Planned German Advance

Expected French Advance

FRANCE

Germany's tactics were based on the Schlieffen Plan. Named after its creator, Count Alfred von Schlieffen. He believed France would be easiest to defeat and Russia would take longer to mobilize their troops. He was wrong on both counts.

In the east, Russia not only mobilized quickly but invaded Prussia. The German army was in retreat until Hindenburg and Ludendorrf took charge. A combination of luck and good tactics helped win the day. The luck was the interception of uncoded Russian radio transmissions.

This gave the Germans the knowledge of Russian troop numbers and positioning. They attacked quickly and, despite being outnumbered, inflicted a devastating blow on the Russian army at the Battle of Tannenberg.

Over half of Russia's 230,000 troops were killed, injured, or captured while the German forces suffered only 20,000 casualties. It was the last time Russian soldiers would set foot on German soil until World War 2.

As the retreat from Mons continued, my brother Joe was amongst those troops forced to hold a rear guard action to buy time for their comrades to escape to safety.

You two, what in blazes are you still doing here? You should have retreated half an hour ago!

Quick, the map showed an orchard this way. It'll get us back to the battalion.

The Germans! They're closing in!

Didn't expect the barbed wire...

Come on, we'll have to risk it.

Let's get to the door!

BOOM!

Look out!

It's locked!

Not for long.

Captain, you're hurt. Let's try and find some bandages.

No time. Let's get to safety and then we can worry about this little scratch.

The Allies spent weeks retreating mostly with no food or rest...

There they are. We've made it. Thanks, Captain. Looks like you saved us.

He saved *us*...

We couldn't save him though. Poor blighter's done for. Shrapnel in his leg. He's bled out.

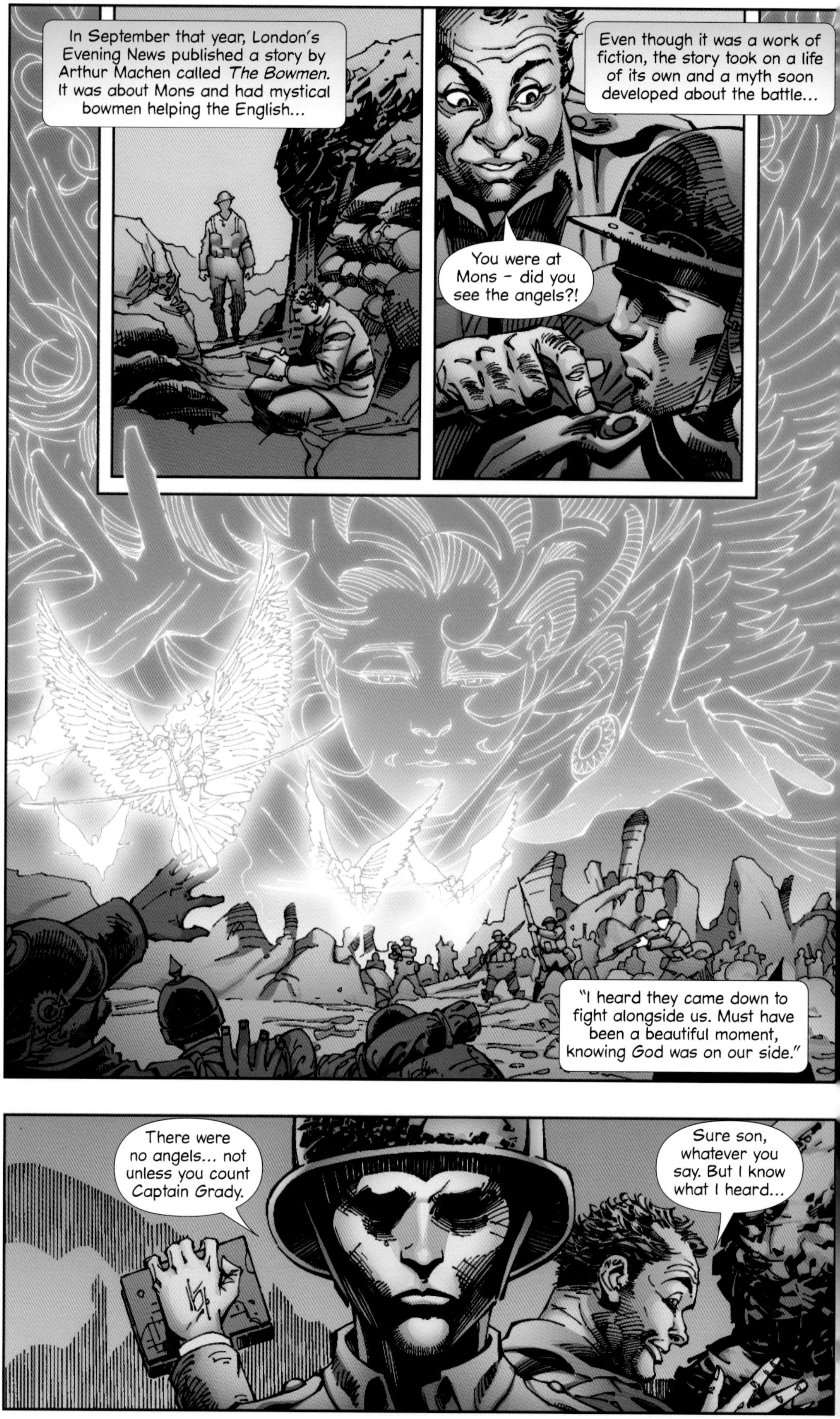
In September that year, London's Evening News published a story by Arthur Machen called *The Bowmen*. It was about Mons and had mystical bowmen helping the English...
Even though it was a work of fiction, the story took on a life of its own and a myth soon developed about the battle...
You were at Mons - did you see the angels?!
"I heard they came down to fight alongside us. Must have been a beautiful moment, knowing God was on our side."
There were no angels... not unless you count Captain Grady.
Sure son, whatever you say. But I know what I heard...

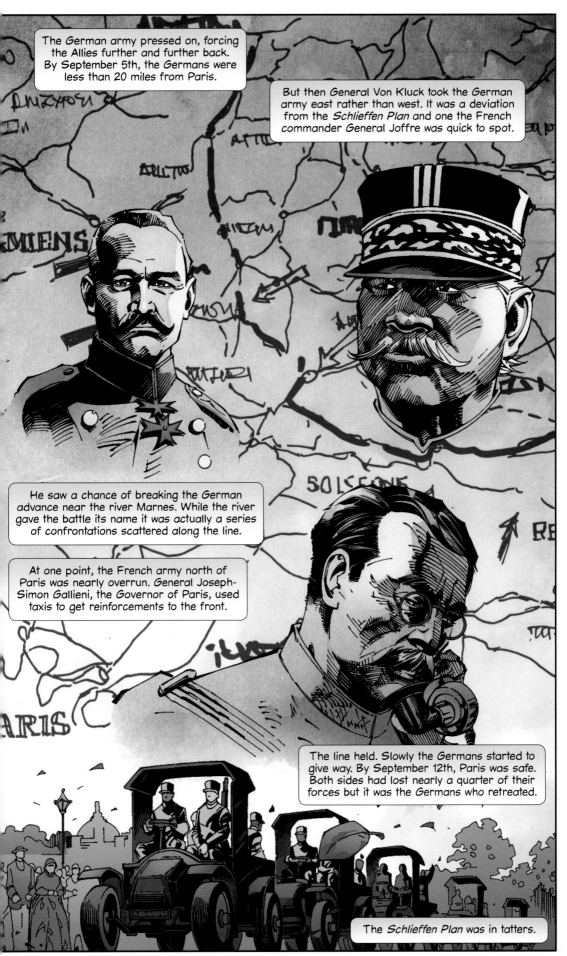

The German army pressed on, forcing the Allies further and further back. By September 5th, the Germans were less than 20 miles from Paris.

But then General Von Kluck took the German army east rather than west. It was a deviation from the *Schlieffen Plan* and one the French commander General Joffre was quick to spot.

He saw a chance of breaking the German advance near the river Marnes. While the river gave the battle its name it was actually a series of confrontations scattered along the line.

At one point, the French army north of Paris was nearly overrun. General Joseph-Simon Gallieni, the Governor of Paris, used taxis to get reinforcements to the front.

The line held. Slowly the Germans started to give way. By September 12th, Paris was safe. Both sides had lost nearly a quarter of their forces but it was the Germans who retreated.

The *Schlieffen Plan* was in tatters.

October saw Joe and his battalion arrive at Ypres as the so-called 'race for the sea' neared its conclusion.

Nice city. Shame war's heading this way.

Following Marnes, the German plan was to reach the ports and thus gain all-important control of the Channel. The Allied plan was simple enough — stop them.

The Allies dug in around the ancient city of Ypres. It was the last chance to stop the German advance.

Welcome to the trenches, son. Got a welcome present for you. These'll give Jerry a shock when they come calling.

Made it out of a milk tin. Maybe we'll get some decent hand grenades before the war's over. Though I won't hold my breath.

Thanks. Bit noisy around here.

Just the shelling. You get used to it. It's when they stop you should worry.

NESTLÉ MILK

Hey, the shelling's stopped. Nice to get some peace and quiet at last!

Stan, what are you doing – get your head down.

THOK!

Stan!!

Sorry, son. He's in a better place now.

We were at Mons together. He saved my life more than once...

Not many of us left now. Reckon that's why we call ourselves the Old Contemptibles.

The what?

The Old Contemptibles. The story goes that we were annoying the Kaiser – what with there being so few of us and still giving Jerry a bloody nose.

I am tired of Sir John French's contemptible little army!

I like that. Hey, Jerry – here's a present from an old contemptible!

That's the spirit, son... Wait a minu-

Get down!

BOOM!

Welcome back, soldier.

Where am I?

Field hospital. There was an explosion but you're safe now. You got lucky. Just a bit of concussion and a few scratches.

The others?

Not so lucky. You were the only one to make it out in one piece.

I am sorry for your loss.

Thanks.

I am Khudadad Khan of the 129th Baluchis.

Joe Smith. So what happened to you?

Now that is quite a story...

The Germans launched a major push at Gheluvelt. We were outnumbered but we gave them a good show.

We're the 129th Baluchis. You will not pass!

"We held the enemy back as long as we could. Eventually I was the only one left..."

"I must have been knocked out because the next thing I remember, the Germans had overrun us."

Leave him. He's dead.

"I spent the night trying to make it back. I was lucky."

Khan reporting for... <Koff>... duty, sir.

He's being modest. He held his position all day – even though he was severely injured.

If it wasn't for him, we'd all be German prisoners by now. Or worse.

Khan became the first member of the Indian army to receive the VC, the British army's highest honor.

Any news from the front?

The weather's getting worse. Soon it'll be too bad for fighting.

The Germans must be getting desperate too. I swear their soldiers seem to be getting younger.

BEI TREIEN ARMEE
DIENEN IHREM LAND

Khan was right. The German army had pushed student volunteers to the frontline. Most had only eight weeks training.

They didn't stand a chance.

Their tragic deaths became known as *Kindermord bei Ypern* or the Massacre of the Innocents in Ypres.

Joe remained away from the frontline for a month. By the time he returned the First Battle of Ypres had ground to a halt, both sides becoming entrenched in their positions.

Elsewhere the war was continuing its bloody work. While Great Britain's Navy was second to none, Germany had been building a fleet of their own in the run up to the war.

The Allies had some good fortune early on when Russian forces captured German codebooks from the *SMS Magdeburg*, a grounded German ship. The Russians passed the codebooks on to the British. The Germans never realized the Allies had their codes until 1918.

The Japanese helped us mop up most of Germany's colonies in the Pacific.

One of the main German successes was Captain Maximilian von Spee. For several months, von Spee's fleet attacked Allied shipping in the Far East before moving to the South Pacific and inflicting a bitter defeat on the Allies at the Battle of Coronel.

The Allied response was to send out two battle cruisers – the *HMS Invincible* and the *HMS Inflexible*. Von Spee was lured into a trap and ordered, by a fake communication, to attack Port Stanley.

The Battle of the Falkland Islands took place on December 8th, 1914. Von Spee's forces were outmatched and destroyed. Von Spee and his two sons died in the battle, together with 1,871 German sailors.

By Christmas 1914, the war had entered a stalemate, with the whole of the western front becoming one vast fortified trench.

Wonder how long these trenches go on for?

From the coast all the way to Switzerland is what I've heard.

Stille Nacht, heilige Nacht...

Never thought I'd spend Christmas in a place like this.

Think it's driving me nuts too. I swear I can hear the Germans singing Silent Night.

I can hear it too. Maybe it's a trick.

It's the Germans, Joe. They've only gone and put Christmas trees up on their side.

And a great big sign that says "Happy Christmas, Tommy!"

There's been no shooting all day. I'm going to wish them Happy Christmas back!

Don't, they'll shoot you!

Nah. Only the generals want us to kill each other at Christmas!

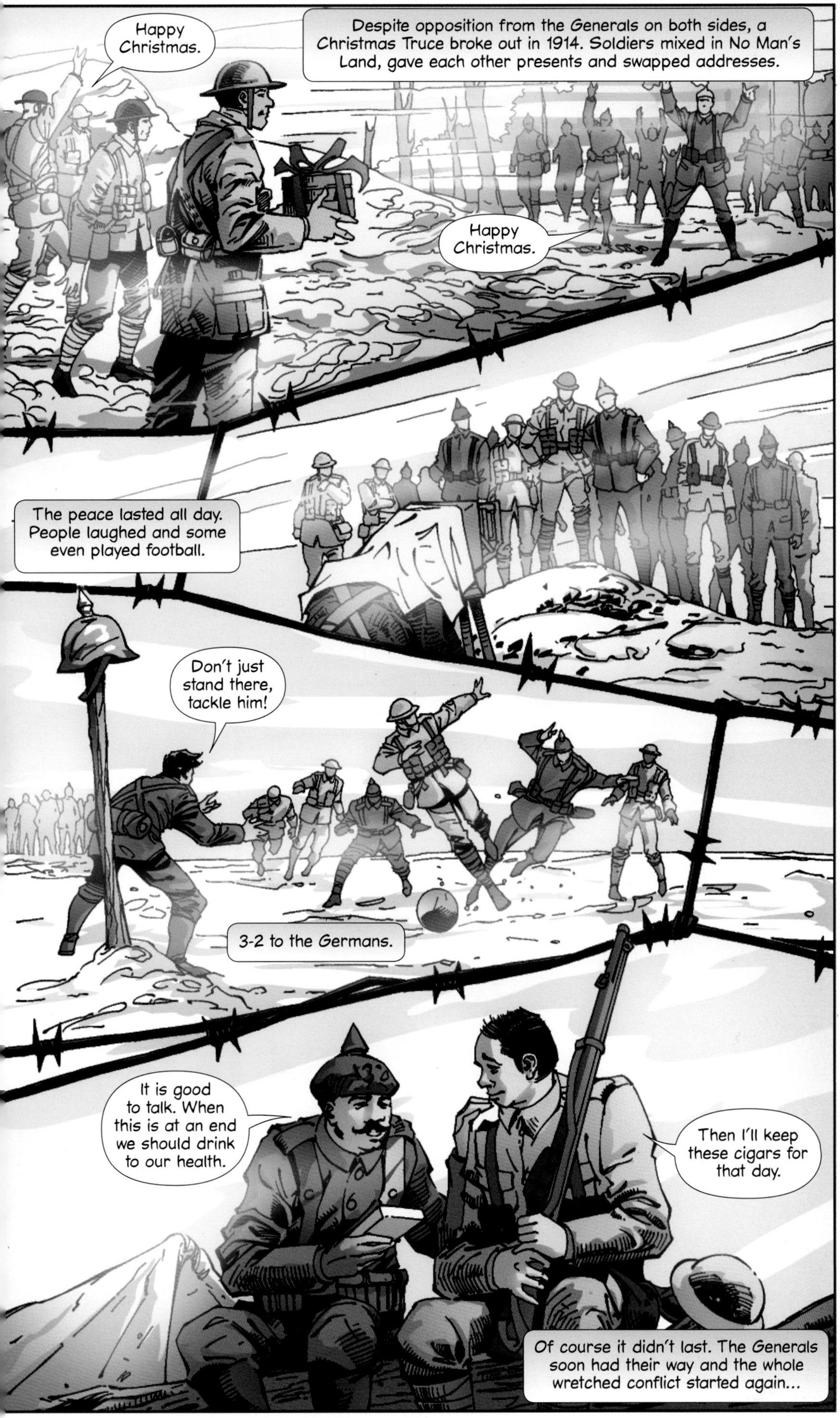
Happy Christmas.
Despite opposition from the Generals on both sides, a Christmas Truce broke out in 1914. Soldiers mixed in No Man's Land, gave each other presents and swapped addresses.
Happy Christmas.
The peace lasted all day. People laughed and some even played football.
Don't just stand there, tackle him!
3-2 to the Germans.
It is good to talk. When this is at an end we should drink to our health.
Then I'll keep these cigars for that day.
Of course it didn't last. The Generals soon had their way and the whole wretched conflict started again...

As 1915 started, people at home were still in the dark about the grim reality of the war.

Winter in the trenches was not a nice experience and something I would suffer through myself by the end of the year.

1915 saw the first zeppelin raids when the Germans bombed Great Yarmouth and King's Lynn.

They even made it to London that May. 35 people were killed in that one.

On December 24th, 1914, the first bombing raid on Britain had taken place. A German pilot, Lt. Prondzynski, tried to destroy Dover Castle.

He threw a bomb by hand from his plane. It missed but injured James Bank who was working in the garden at St James Rectory.

That May saw Joe and his battalion returning to Ypres as the Germans pressed on the city again.

It's changed a bit...

Yeah, looks like war doesn't agree with the place.

With all the practice they'd had, they dug into their new positions quickly.

Smith, time for a water run.

Yes sir.

Joe got lucky. He was at a farmhouse getting water for the troops when the attack began.

Here they come. Looks like Jerry's guns must be falling short – look at all that smoke!

I don't think that's smoke...

It's gas!

Pee on the masks, it's supposed to help stop the gas...

The Second Battle of Ypres was the first time the Germans used gas on the British.

I don't know if I can do that. Sounds disgusting.

Would you rather die?

Pee it is then.

Joe had started to get to know a bloke by the name of Peter Almond. He was 26 and hoped to work in the theater when he got home.

Peter told me that it was at that moment he thought he was done for.

The gas soon melted away but it had done its terrible work. For once the Germans didn't press their advance...

Cleaning the trenches was one of the worst jobs. Especially when the bodies belonged to your friends.

If I hadn't been sent to get water, I'd have been one of these...

Peter? Help!! We've got a live one!!

Peter had been knocked out and fallen back – his pals, his dead pals, had fallen on top of him creating a small air pocket and keeping the worst of the gas away from him.

Come on, let's get you out of here. We'll get you to the stage yet.

Peter survived the war and ended up managing the local theater back home. He had a good life. Guess he really was one of the lucky ones.

Gas was first used at the Second Battle of Ypres. Early attacks relied on the wind to blow the gas over the enemy positions.

Different types of gas were soon brought into play, including phosgene and mustard gas. 91,000 men were killed by gas while those injured numbered as many as 3,000,000.

Not long after the fighting at Ypres, Joe actually got leave. He was heading back to Blighty just as we were getting shipped out to Flanders!

Once we got to France a surprise was waiting for us – a load of old London buses to take us part of the way.

It was a strange business seeing London buses covered in mud and dirt and filled with soldiers.

We were with the 8th Battalion of the Rifleman's. There was yet more training...

But before we knew it we were at the front.

You okay, Fred? You've been awfully quiet of late.

Can I tell you a secret?

I don't want to kill anyone. Not even a Jerry...

I'm scared. I'm scared that I'll die. That I'll never see my brother, Alfie, again. I'm scared that I might have to kill someone...

Reckon when it's time you won't have a choice. Bet you don't even have time to think about it...

You two. Outside now. Got a little job for you.

Nice bit of wiring needs to be done. You come from a wire town, don't you? Should be a breeze.

Keep your heads down and try not to get shot. Good lads.

Wiring parties were terrifying experiences. A group would go out into No Man's Land between the trenches at night to fix the defenses or even build new ones.

Got a feeling he doesn't like us.

Got a feeling he doesn't like anyone.

It was dangerous work. The slightest sound could result in death.

Both sides sent flares up through the night to illuminate No Man's Land – and hopefully take their enemies by surprise.

Flare!

If it wasn't for Fred hearing the flare go up, we'd have been caught standing in the middle of No Man's Land and shot to bits.

We had to lie on the ground as flat as we could, hoping the Germans didn't spot us...

As it was, poor Phil Eddolls was too late to find cover.

BLAM

There was nothing we could do for him, except pray.

It wasn't quick work either. We were out there for over two hours. You tried not to think of what could happen but sometimes you couldn't help yourself.

Eddolls got hit. He's still out there.

Can't be helped, he'll just have to stay where he is. Now go get some kip. You deserve it.

It was while we were away from the front line that we heard about the sinking of the RMS Lusitania.

It was one of the biggest ships in the world. She left New York bound for Liverpool on May 1st, 1915 only to be torpedoed by a German U-Boat on May 7th, just off the coast of Ireland. She sank in just 18 minutes, claiming the lives of 1,198 people – including 128 Americans.

News of the attack outraged the United States and, for a while, we felt sure America would enter the war on our side... but they didn't and remained neutral for another two years.

While I was trying to get used to life in the trenches, Joe was trying to get used to life back in Blighty.

At the time there was a spate of girls giving people white feathers. Always found the idea distasteful myself. If you want to fight you fight. If you don't...

Excuse me, sir. We have a little present for you. As you're so brave...

Well, some people aren't cut out for war and those who think they are soon change their mind when they get to the front.

...especially with all the real men at war.

Ladies, I've just returned from Ypres where I saw my best friend blown to bits in front of me. I've seen men...

Well, let's just say I've seen things that shouldn't be seen.

So next time you consider accosting people in the street, perhaps you should think twice. Good day.

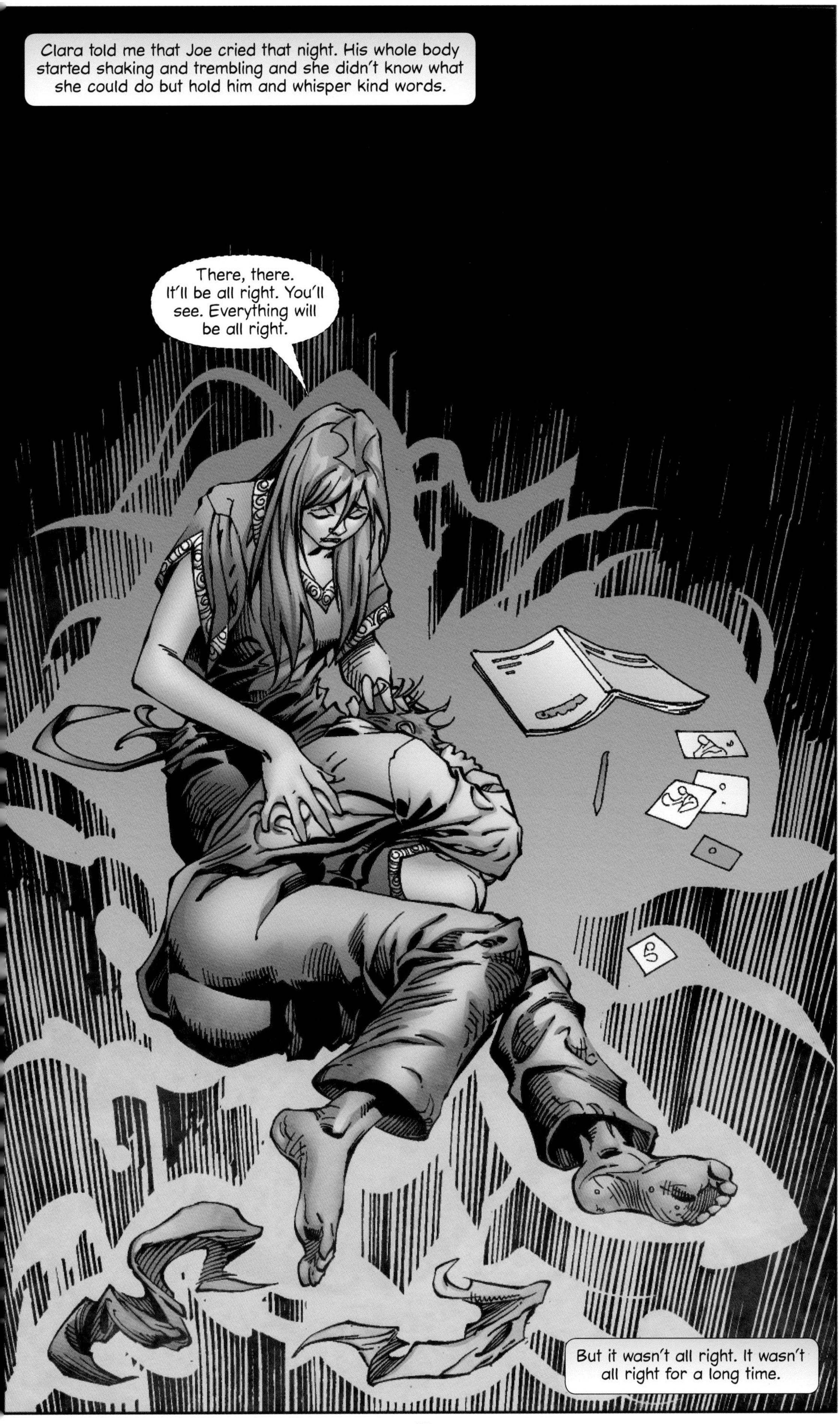
Clara told me that Joe cried that night. His whole body started shaking and trembling and she didn't know what she could do but hold him and whisper kind words.
There, there. It'll be all right. You'll see. Everything will be all right.
But it wasn't all right. It wasn't all right for a long time.

That July, the British had captured the small town of Hooge, which was a small village two miles east of Ypres.

BOOM!

British sappers had dug under the German positions and planted explosives. The blast was greater than anyone had expected and created a huge crater, killing several hundred German soldiers in the process.

On July 31st, our battalion was sent in to relieve those in the trenches on the edge of the crater...

Not much of a view is it?

Not much of a trench either, bit too close to Jerry for my liking.

Did you hear that?

Hear what?

Get down, they're shelling!

BOOM!

BOOM!

ARRRGGH!

The Battle of Hooge saw the Germans unleash a new weapon...

...the flamethrower.

VROOSH

Liquid fire was sprayed over our trench, causing chaos, mayhem and death.

The German onslaught started at 3.15 AM and it was my battalion that took the brunt of attack.

Captain!

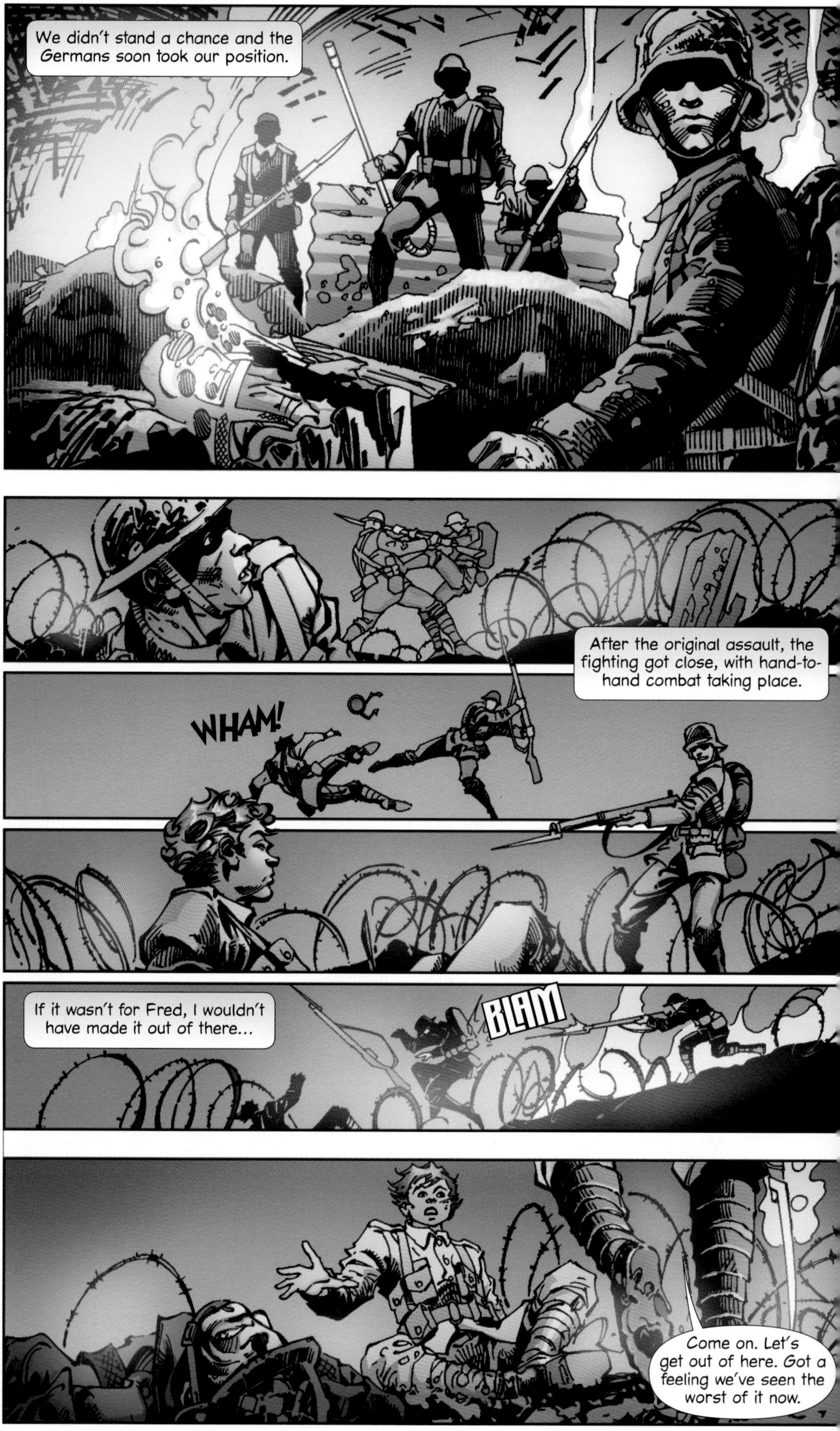

We didn't stand a chance and the Germans soon took our position.
After the original assault, the fighting got close, with hand-to-hand combat taking place.
WHAM!
If it wasn't for Fred, I wouldn't have made it out of there...
BLAM
Come on. Let's get out of here. Got a feeling we've seen the worst of it now.

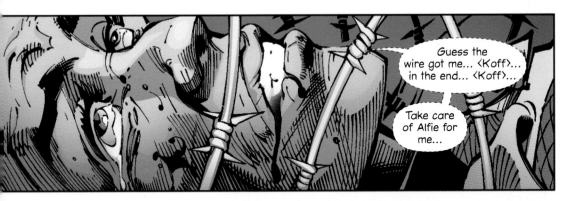

Guess the wire got me... ⟨Koff⟩... in the end... ⟨Koff⟩...

Take care of Alfie for me...

Fred Cowsill was the closest friend I ever had. A day doesn't go by when I don't think of him...

When I don't miss him...

I'd be lying if I said I was myself after that day.

The following weeks went by in a blur.

Smith, show the newcomers the ropes and watch their backs.

Don't look over the trench or you'll be blown to bits, you idiot!

A month or so after we lost Hooge to the Germans, new recruits started to arrive. We'd been part of Kitchener's first wave but now felt like old hands compared to the fresh-faced kids turning up.

Keep your head down and try not to get shot.

I don't think he likes us...

That September they were about to have their baptism of fire at the battle of Loos.

The Battle of Loos started on September 23rd. It was the first time the British used gas... but the wind blew it back onto our own ranks...

Still the fellows fought bravely but as usual their leaders let them down with bad planning and bad supply lines.

The Germans killed so many of Kitchener's new army their title for the battle became "the Field of Corpses of Loos".

The one good thing that came out of it was the replacement of Field Marshal French. Never had much faith in him. But then again by that point I didn't have much faith in any of the generals.

The war left a lot of us with a dislike of generals. I met an Aussie vet years later who'd fought at Gallipoli. He hated them with a passion.

Gallipoli was an attempt by the Allies to break through Turkish lines and take Constantinople but indecision, bad communication and tough opposition coupled with the landings occurring in the wrong places made it a disastrous operation.

The landings on April 25th became a massacre. Brave Australian and New Zealand soldiers died as the warzone soon became yet another bloody stalemate.

The Allies lost about 265,000 men, while the Turkish forces suffered casualties of about 218,000 men.

The Allies withdrew ten months later with nothing to show for the campaign but thousands of dead.

April 25th became known as ANZAC Day to the Australians and New Zealanders. A national day of remembrance...

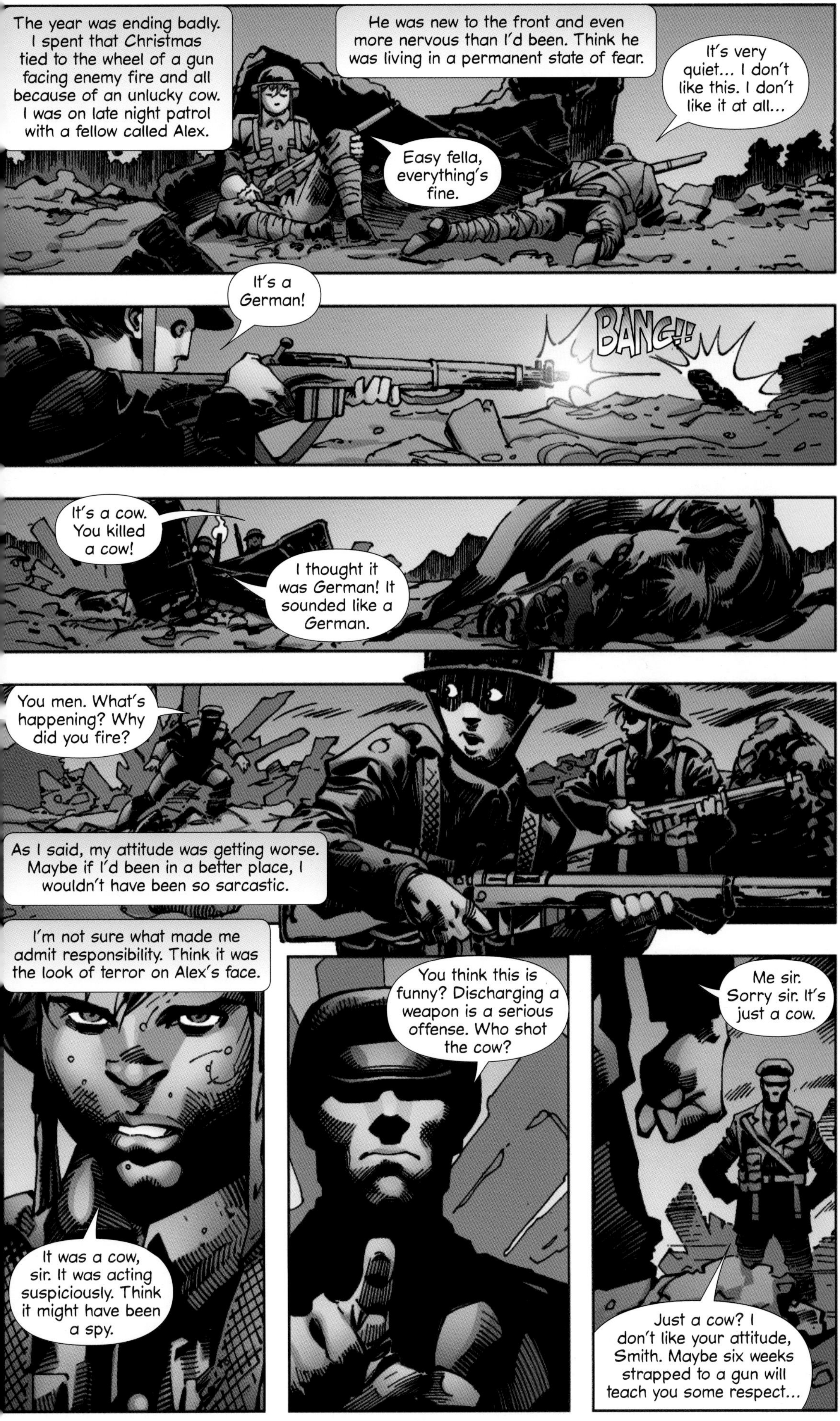
The year was ending badly. I spent that Christmas tied to the wheel of a gun facing enemy fire and all because of an unlucky cow. I was on late night patrol with a fellow called Alex.
He was new to the front and even more nervous than I'd been. Think he was living in a permanent state of fear.
It's very quiet... I don't like this. I don't like it at all...
Easy fella, everything's fine.
It's a German!
BANG!!
It's a cow. You killed a cow!
I thought it was German! It sounded like a German.
You men. What's happening? Why did you fire?
As I said, my attitude was getting worse. Maybe if I'd been in a better place, I wouldn't have been so sarcastic.
I'm not sure what made me admit responsibility. Think it was the look of terror on Alex's face.
It was a cow, sir. It was acting suspiciously. Think it might have been a spy.
You think this is funny? Discharging a weapon is a serious offense. Who shot the cow?
Me sir. Sorry sir. It's just a cow.
Just a cow? I don't like your attitude, Smith. Maybe six weeks strapped to a gun will teach you some respect...

Field Punishment Number One meant I was tied to a gun for two hours a day for two weeks.

The Captain must have liked me because he put me just out of reach of German bullets. I heard some fellas weren't as lucky...

Joe told me that the previous Christmas had been wondrous. That people from both sides met and shared presents.

The generals made sure that didn't happen again. They wanted war and war was what they got.

It was a bad Christmas but worse was to come. The following year we moved positions...

...to the Somme.

The start of 1916 saw conscription hit *Great Britain* as thousands of young men were called up for the war.

In Russia, discontent was growing while in Germany the British sea blockade was starting to affect the everyday life of the German people, with food and other essentials running low.

The year started off okay. At least once the army had stopped crucifying me for two hours a day.

Thanks for taking the blame. I don't think I could have handled that...

All the lads reckon you're a hero. Apart from Cockney Mike who thinks you're mad.

Tea for you, George. Extra chlorine, just how you like it.

Lovely.

For some of us, black humor was all that got us through the day. All the water we used had chlorine added, it was the only way to make it fit to drink...

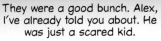

They were a good bunch. Alex, I've already told you about. He was just a scared kid.

Little John was a bit of a scoundrel but fun with it. Used to tell some of the dirtiest jokes I'd ever heard.

Danny Boy was a nice bloke. Came from Ireland and was mad about the place...

Big John was a rugby player and built like a shed. One of the strongest and nicest blokes I've ever met.

Cockney Mike was from South London. He used to work on a fair back home and was pretty handy at making things work.

Mornin' Smith. At ease.

Heard what you did for young Alex. Took guts that did.

Don't know what you mean, sir.

'Course you don't, son. Anyway, Smith. The fellas need your help trying to get the new field gun in place.

...and I've got a little surprise for you.

Joe!

All right, George. What's this I hear about you getting in trouble?

Only what you taught me!

Couldn't believe it when I heard they were transferring me to your regiment. Cracking spot of luck.

Okay, ladies. We have work to do.

Seems one of the cows has took a real liking to the spot we need to place the gun and is refusing to move.

Don't shoot, Smith. It's a British cow!

We spent hours trying to move the cow. When we eventually did everyone cheered. It was a good day. One of the last we had for a long time.

Elsewhere, the Battle of Verdun had started. The battle raged from February 21st and was one of the most brutal the French took part in.

The German plan was simple – throw their soldiers into battle and make the French army 'bleed to death'.

The battle lasted until the end of the year with both sides taking more than 300,000 casualties.

Meanwhile, We'd had a quiet few months and suspected our luck was going to run out.

We moved to new positions near the Somme a couple of weeks before the Big Push.

Time for a changeover, Danny boy.

Ace, I'm dying for the loo.

Snipers.

KRACK!

Danny!

At least it was quick.

There was a routine to life in the trenches. We'd rise before dawn – in case the enemy attacked – and then 'the Morning Hate' began, when both sides shot at each other.

BLAM

BLAM

BLAM

Nice day for a war.

Then we'd clean our kit – tricky with so much dirt around.

And then we'd all sit down for breakfast...

What is it today?

Same muck as yesterday with an added dollop of grease and some lovely stale bread.

Can I have your bread? It's so hard it makes a great art-board.

After what passed for food, we'd get to work on trench repairs.

Still want a life of high adventure?

I do miss the farm on occasion.

I miss your farm and I've never been there!

Dusk saw a stand-at-arms again as it was thought just before dawn and dusk were the key times the enemy could attack.

Damn! Why is it always me?!

As darkness fell, other jobs could take place – such as cleaning out the toilets...

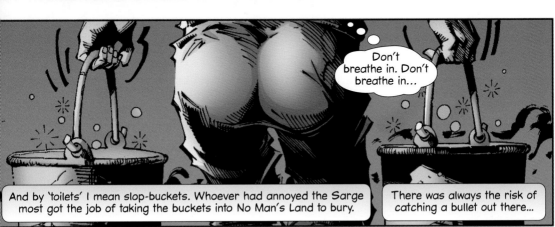

Don't breathe in. Don't breathe in...

And by 'toilets' I mean slop-buckets. Whoever had annoyed the Sarge most got the job of taking the buckets into No Man's Land to bury.

There was always the risk of catching a bullet out there...

Easy does it, Mike. Just a few more steps and we're do--

OH SHI--

BLOP!

...but sometimes, there are worse things than just being shot.

The main sea battle of the war took place off the coast of Jutland, Denmark on May 31st, 1916. The Commander of the German High Seas Fleet, Reinhardt Scheer, had started to attack British forces once again but was unaware that the British were in possession of German codes.

When he launched a massive attack on the British coast, the HMS *Indefatigable* was sunk and the *Queen Mary* blown up — but the Germans were sailing into a trap.

The British Sea Commander, Admiral Jellicoe, was waiting for him and the German ships were suddenly at the mercy of the British dreadnoughts. The Germans escaped just in time.

The British sunk the *Lutzow* but, as Scheer ordered a vast torpedo attack, retreated to avoid greater damage. That night the German fleet escaped.

The battle was inconclusive. The Germans sank more ships but the British were ready for more fighting. The Germans never risked their armada again, returning to attacks by U-boats. A policy that would eventually help bring America into the war.

By the end of June we all knew a big push was coming on the Somme. Our guns had been blasting away at the German lines for seven days.

Our artillery will have torn the German defenses to shreds. The barbed wire will have been destroyed and the trenches will be in ruins.

You know, I'm not sure I believe him.

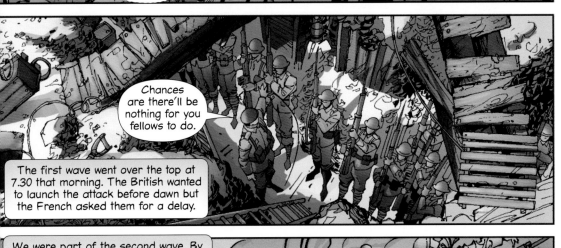

Chances are there'll be nothing for you fellows to do.

The first wave went over the top at 7.30 that morning. The British wanted to launch the attack before dawn but the French asked them for a delay.

We were part of the second wave. By that time, the explosions and gunfire were telling us that the Germans were very much still there and ready for us.

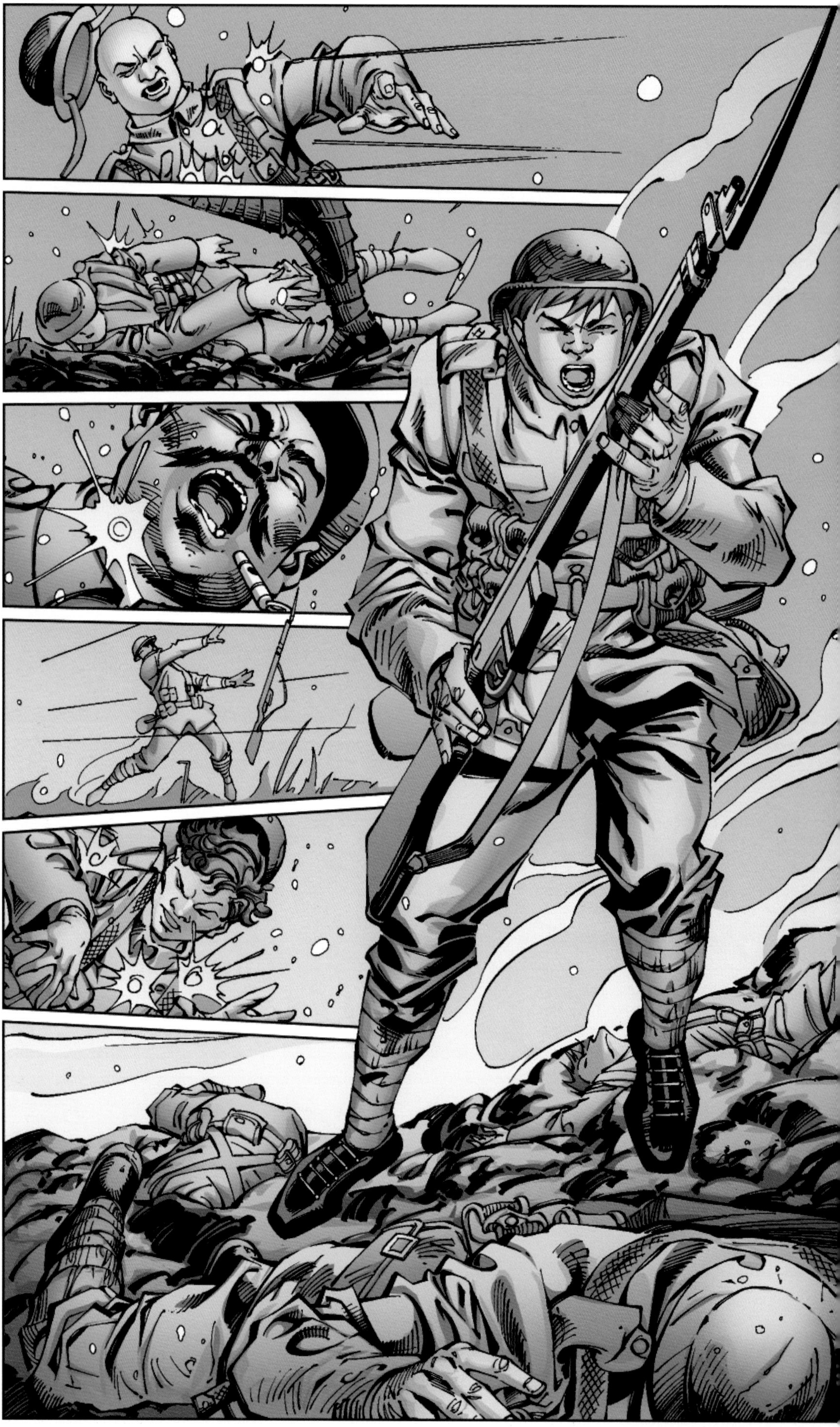

BOOM!

The first day of the Somme became the bloodiest day in British military history. The army suffered 57,470 casualties with 19,240 killed or dying through injuries.

Contrary to what the British hoped, their bombardment had failed and the German trenches were still intact. Their machine guns cut through the British line as it rained bullets.

RATATAA

The fighting lasted until November and resulted in 127,751 British casualties for an advance of only seven miles.

The Germans also suffered mass casualties with between 465,000 to 680,000 killed and injured during the offensive.

Most of my friends were among those who died on that hellish day.

Some battalions tried to ease the fear by throwing a football into No Man's Land and following it across the killing fields...

Come on lads, let's have a kick around!

Many towns and cities lost an entire generation of men as the Pals Battalions were mowed down.

These battalions consisted of friends and colleagues from a small village or factory who fought together and died together.

Some were hit harder than others. The Newfoundlanders endured ninety-one per cent casualties with 658 of 726 men injured or killed.

Georgie boy!

If I hadn't stumbled, the bullets that claimed Cockney Mike would have had my name on them.

As it was, I nearly didn't make it.

You're not going to die. You're not going to die. You're not going to die.

BOOM!

Bad place for a kip.

Come on, lads. One last push.

Some of the fellas are already in the German trenches!

BLAM BLAM

Captain!

George, what are you doing, you'll get shot!

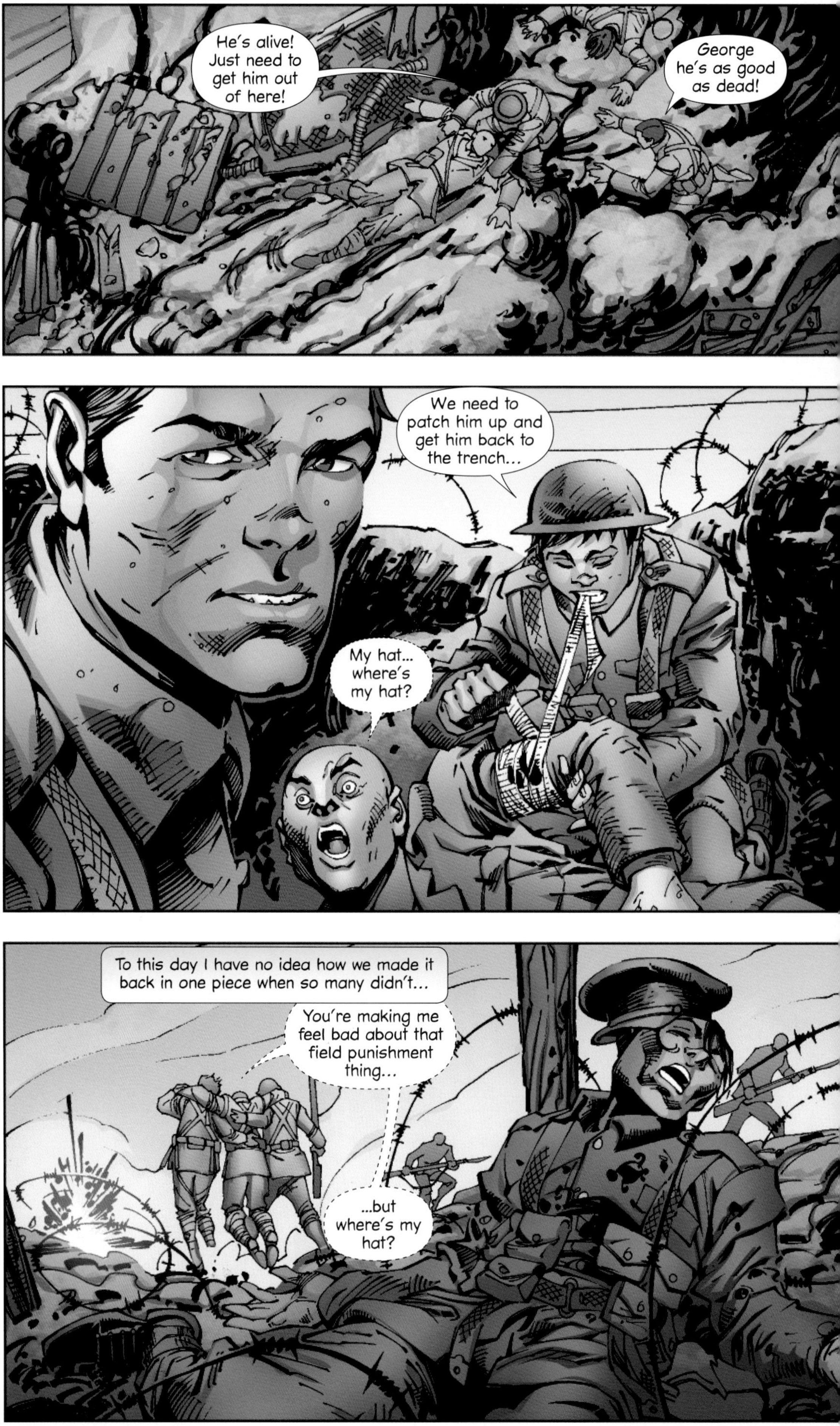
He's alive! Just need to get him out of here!
George he's as good as dead!
We need to patch him up and get him back to the trench...
My hat... where's my hat?
To this day I have no idea how we made it back in one piece when so many didn't...
You're making me feel bad about that field punishment thing...
...but where's my hat?

That September, the Allies put a terrifying new weapon in the field — the tank!

Originally called Landships, a prototype tank named 'Big Willie' had been tested early in 1916 and they first saw action on September 15th.

Der Teufel kommt!!*

The monstrous new combat vehicles terrified the Germans and, while one third of them broke down, they were largely responsible for pushing the Germans out of the village of Flers.

*The Devil is coming!!

By the end of 1916, people back home had started to realize the terrible truth of the war as the papers became filled with lists of the dead.

I'm so sorry.

John. My poor little John.

On December 12th the Germans sent a peace note to the allies, suggesting a compromise.

However neither side would have been able to claim a 'victory' and too many lives had been lost to think of compromising now.

Apart from me and Joe, only Alex of my old friends survived those cruel months.

Too many had died on both sides. Young lives thrown away for no real reason. For just a few miles of mud.

And by the end of the year the Germans had already started to retrench their forces in what would become known as the Hindenburg Line...

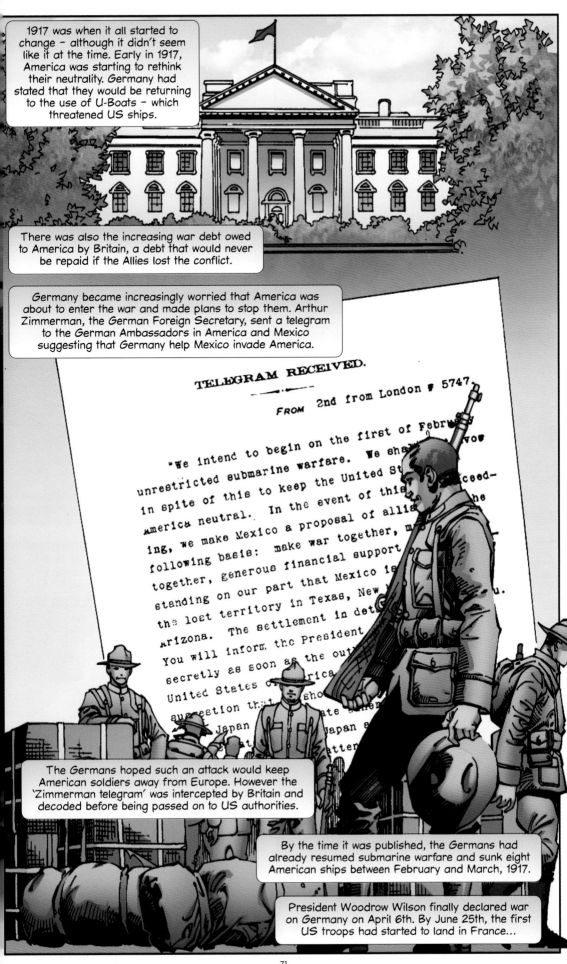

1917 was when it all started to change – although it didn't seem like it at the time. Early in 1917, America was starting to rethink their neutrality. Germany had stated that they would be returning to the use of U-Boats – which threatened US ships.

There was also the increasing war debt owed to America by Britain, a debt that would never be repaid if the Allies lost the conflict.

Germany became increasingly worried that America was about to enter the war and made plans to stop them. Arthur Zimmerman, the German Foreign Secretary, sent a telegram to the German Ambassadors in America and Mexico suggesting that Germany help Mexico invade America.

TELEGRAM RECEIVED.

FROM 2nd from London # 5747

"We intend to begin on the first of Febru unrestricted submarine warfare. We sha in spite of this to keep the United St ceed- America neutral. In the event of this he ing, we make Mexico a proposal of allia following basis: make war together, m together, generous financial support standing on our part that Mexico is the lost territory in Texas, New Arizona. The settlement in det u. You will inform the President secretly as soon as the out United States rica suggestion that sho ate Japan Japan tten

The Germans hoped such an attack would keep American soldiers away from Europe. However the 'Zimmerman telegram' was intercepted by Britain and decoded before being passed on to US authorities.

By the time it was published, the Germans had already resumed submarine warfare and sunk eight American ships between February and March, 1917.

President Woodrow Wilson finally declared war on Germany on April 6th. By June 25th, the first US troops had started to land in France...

Back on the frontline, I'd gained a promotion and an actual bed to sleep in.

Even if I had to share it with the odd unwanted visitor...

You know, Joe, I swear these rats are getting bigger.

Good. We'll stew it. Now go back to sleep.

It was hard to sleep though – especially with everything we'd seen.

Some nights I could hear the screams of my fallen friends.

Don't worry George, you'll be joining us soon enough.

It was on those bad nights that Martha's picture kept me alive.

Don't worry, George. One day this'll all be over and you'll be with her again. It'll be okay. It'll all be okay...

It was getting to everyone. Some more than others.

I can't take it anymore. Please make it stop.

Easy, Alex. We'll be fine...

He's not been the same since Danny got it.

We also had some new guys. My favorite was Davy Fletcher. He was a mad fella, full of himself with a great laugh.

Don't know how he did it. They kicked him out of the Royal Flying Corps and sent him to the front line.

He'd loved the Flying Corps and I think leaving it had broken his heart... he was always going on about it...

You want to know about planes? I'll tell you about planes...

I never thought I'd be a flyboy, see? I wasn't posh enough.

"A lot of the early fliers had learned before the war in their own planes. I got in as a mechanic but managed to talk my way into the air pretty quickly."

"It was all very civilized at the start of the war. Pilots on both sides even waved at each other when they passed in the skies..."

Good flying weather!

"We did an important job too. From spotting the enemy to mapping out their positions and trench layouts..."

"And I tell you, there's nothing like being high in the sky, flying through the clouds..."

"Even when some blighter's trying to shoot you."

"It wasn't half dangerous though. Our noble leaders thought parachutes might make us abandon the plane too quickly."

"With the fuel tank underneath the seats in some models, it could be a nasty way to go..."

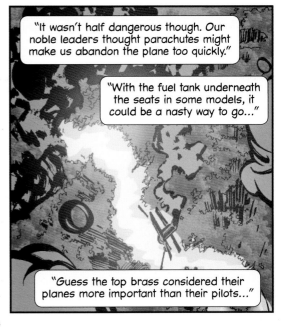

"Guess the top brass considered their planes more important than their pilots..."

I wasn't the only one getting cynical. The French had had it just as bad as us lot if not worse.

Robert Nivelle had replaced Joffre as their new commander in 1916 and claimed to have come up with the idea of the creeping barrage. This was a decent enough battle tactic where a barrage of artillery would take place just in front of an infantry advance.

The tactic failed abysmally though during the Spring Offensive along the river Aisne. The French suffered 130,000 casualties. It was the last straw for many French soldiers and they mutinied.

For a while it looked like France might go the way of Russia, who were having a revolution of their own, but Nivelle was replaced by Marshal Philippe Petain, and his tactics seemed much more suited to the situation.

He managed to quell the uprising using a mixture of toughness and efficiency. Some of the soldiers were sent to Devil's Island as punishment while at least forty-three were executed.

I met a lot of folk during the war that impressed me. Some of the toughest were the tunnellers...

The crater at Hooge was their work. As was the Messines Ridge explosion that June.

The ridge was strategically important as it overlooked the Allied positions. On June 7th, nineteen mines containing 450 tonnes of explosive were detonated beneath German positions.

Over 10,000 Germans died and within a few hours the position was under British control.

They were part of the Royal Engineering Corps, and did amazing – not to mention terrifying – work.

They had all been miners or had helped build the London Underground before the war. They dug tunnels under enemy lines, laid explosives and then blew Jerry to kingdom come!

Sometimes they'd hear the enemy creating their own tunnels nearby and end up fighting each other underground...

If they had a chance, they'd get out and blow the tunnels behind them, burying the enemy miners alive.

That June saw Joe and myself desperate to get home. We had seven days leave all to ourselves.

We left the front line behind, watching others take our place as we sweet talked our way back to Blighty.

Come on, Guv. Just a lift to the coast. We've been at the front...

Okay, hop in. Just be quick about it and don't tell any of your pals. I don't want to become a taxi-service.

We were crossing London on June 13th, little suspecting that Jerry had followed us...

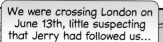

A fleet of twenty aircraft bombed Blighty that morning. The largest bombing raid of the war.

What the...?

A foundry near East London was done in just as we were passing...

Get down!

Instead of a nice, calm holiday we found ourselves rescuing workers from the smoking ruins...

The bombing raids killed 162 people while a further raid on July 7th killed 57 more.

I'm starting to think that the Bosche don't like us.

In case you're worried, we did make it back eventually. Though our Mother wasn't impressed with the state of us!

Get those filthy clothes off before you come in. Your sister's bringing someone from the hospital to clean you both up - I don't want any lice in the house!

Things were changing back home too. Both Martha and Clara had jobs in the local factory...

Jobs men would have done a few years before.

The war had an effect on the farm too.

It's quiet without the horses.

Hope they're okay. Doesn't seem right, the army taking them to war.

The army had bought the horses for the war effort. A shilling each we got for them. They never came back.

Sorry it's not much...

Anything's better than bully beef...

Food was getting short too.

Do you think this horrid war will ever end?

Sure. Sooner rather than later.

Of course I didn't tell Martha that for the whole two days we got to spend back home I could still hear the distant rumbling of the war and the screams of my friends...

The scary truth was that we were starting to feel more at home in the trenches than we did anywhere else...

For the Russians, 1917 was a year of revolution and blood. Their leaders were so vicious – not to mention useless – they made our own lot look good.

Over 1,500,000 Russian soldiers had died by 1917 and the generals were more than willing to send countless more to their doom.

The Tsar had abdicated in February 1917 but the people were still not happy. The workers wanted real social change.

In March, aided by Germany, Vladimir Lenin, leader of the Bolsheviks, returned to Russia from exile in Switzerland. News of his homecoming spread and gave the revolutionaries a rallying point.

By the end of the year, Lenin and the Bolsheviks were the new Russian leaders and had signed an armistice with the Central Powers.

Russia was out of the war, leaving Germany able to focus all their attention on the Western Front.

Luckily for us, the Doughboys were arriving...

On the way back to our unit we met some of the first American soldiers to be sent over.

They looked so hopeful and starry eyed.

So different to the rest of us.

Hey guys, good to meet you. Which way's the war?

The American Commander in Chief, John Pershing, had actually served in the Indian Wars. He wanted to make sure the army was well-trained before it went into action.

When the American Expeditionary Force first arrived a few were attached to British and French units. Four battalions of African American soldiers were incorporated into the French army. The main American force would arrive the following year.

Healthy looking bunch aren't they?

You'd think the locals had never seen a soldier before...

I spent so much time fighting in the mud of the Western Front it was easy to forget the war was happening elsewhere as well.

Some of the toughest fighting took place on the Italian front, where the Italian army, led by General Luigi Cadorna, faced the Austro-Hungarians. A lot of the fighting took place in the foothills of the Alps, close to the River Isonzo.

The Battles of the Isonzo took place between 1915 and 1917. There were twelve separate battles during those years and the last, better known as the Battle of Caporetto, proved costly for the Italians.

The Austrians, backed by seven German divisions, cut through the Italian lines, forcing Cadorna to order a retreat.

While the enemy advance was eventually stopped at the river Piave, it proved to be an embarrassing and costly defeat for the Italians. They lost 40,000 men with 300,000 taken prisoner.

In East Africa, the Allies wanted to capture Germany's colonies but this was easier said than done.

Led by General Paul Emil von Lettow-Vorbeck, the German forces in East Africa held out against a large force of South African troops, as well as the Indian Army, right up until the end of the war. In fact Lettow-Vorberck's undefeated army did not formally surrender until almost two weeks after the Armistice was signed.

When we eventually made it back to the front, Alex seemed to be in a worse state than ever.

Hey, Alex, miss us?

Dennis got it while you were away. Shell came over. Blew him to bits it did. Had bits of him in my hair...

Tell them to stop the shelling. Please. Tell them to stop.

There is no shelling tonight, Alex.

Truth be told, Alex scared me. I couldn't help feeling I was just a few bad days from being just liked him.

I can hear them. I can always hear them. Big Johnny. Little Johnny. I see Danny dying all the time. Right in front of me. It never stops.

It never stops!!

The trauma of fighting and the psychological strain gave rise to 'shell shock', a new condition that many generals and medical officers gave little importance to. It is now better known as 'post-traumatic stress disorder'.

The condition ranged from frayed nerves to complete mental breakdowns. Rather than help the victims, many of the leaders saw them as cowards or 'malingerers'.

For some, it was all too much and they deserted. During the course of the war, 351 men were executed for various crimes – including 268 for desertion. France executed 600 of their own.

Executions were usually carried out at dawn, with soldiers from the victims' own battalion forced to execute their comrade.

Years after the war, the descendants of those wrongly executed sought justice for that terrible wrong. They still do.

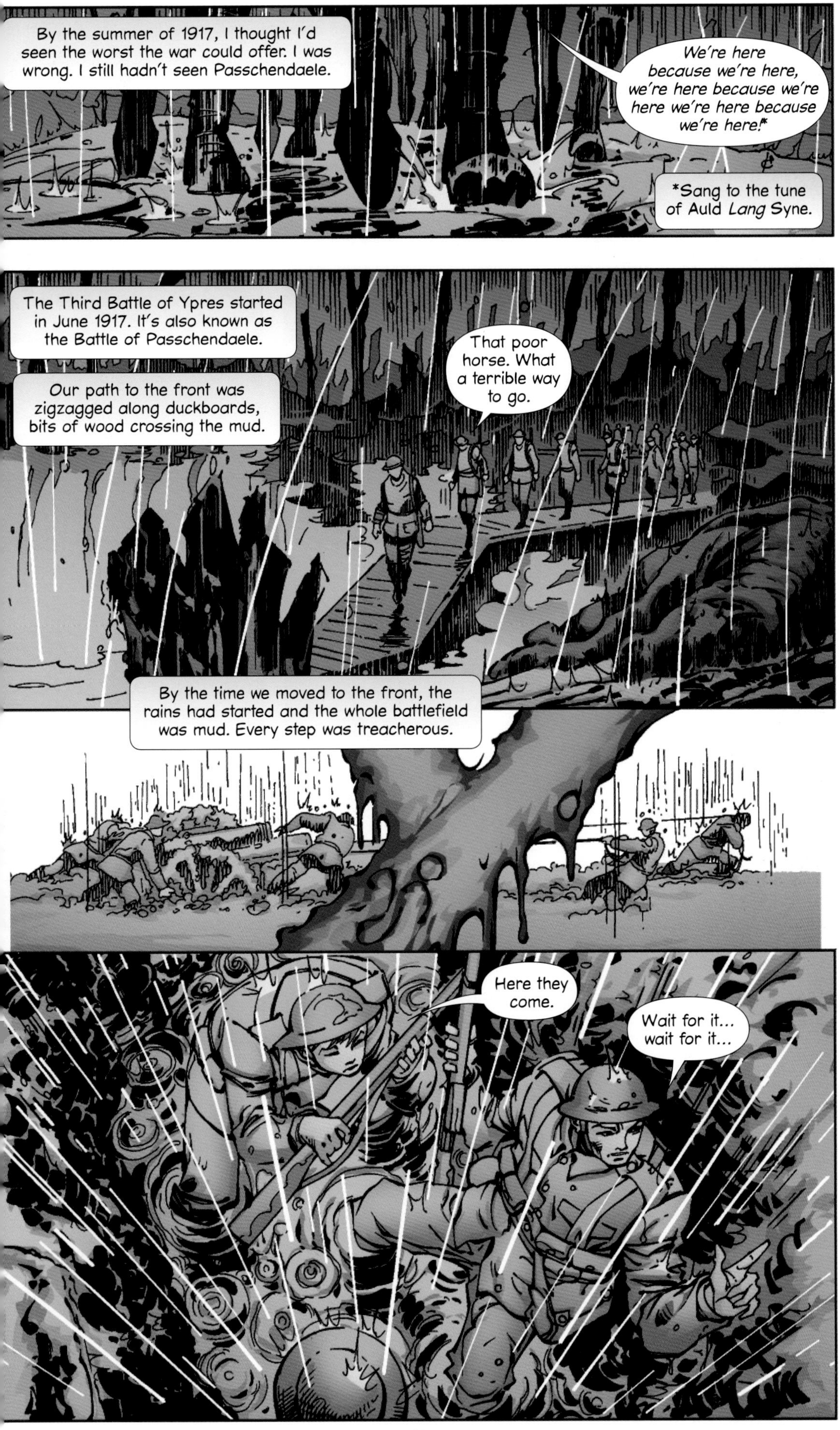

By the summer of 1917, I thought I'd seen the worst the war could offer. I was wrong. I still hadn't seen Passchendaele.
*We're here because we're here, we're here because we're here we're here because we're here!**
*Sang to the tune of Auld *Lang* Syne.
The Third Battle of Ypres started in June 1917. It's also known as the Battle of Passchendaele.
Our path to the front was zigzagged along duckboards, bits of wood crossing the mud.
That poor horse. What a terrible way to go.
By the time we moved to the front, the rains had started and the whole battlefield was mud. Every step was treacherous.
Here they come.
Wait for it... wait for it...

Passchendaele quickly became one of the most notorious battles of the war. British artillery bombarded the enemy for fourteen days...

BLAM BLAM

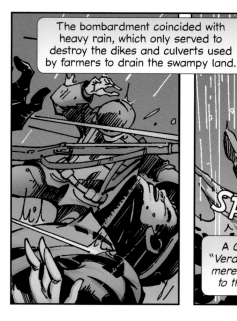

The bombardment coincided with heavy rain, which only served to destroy the dikes and culverts used by farmers to drain the swampy land.

SPLOSH!

A German soldier wrote "Verdun and the Somme are mere purgatories compared to this concentrated Hell."

UFFF!

By the time Canadian and Australian soldiers captured Passchendaele over 240,000 Allied soldiers had died...

BLAM!

The fighting was vicious...

THWACK!

When we ran out of ammo we used our bare hands...

We became animals.

THUNK!

GAK-KKH!

KLIK!

KLIK!

Run.

Some say one in four soldiers drowned in the mud of that hellish battle...

You seen Alex?

No.

We never did find out what happened to poor Alex.

85

1917 proved to be a successful year for the Allies in the Middle East. They enjoyed a series of impressive victories over the Turks, with Baghdad falling to them in March and Jerusalem in December.

The success of the campaign owed a great deal to an Arab uprising inspired by one man – the legendary Colonel T. E. Lawrence, who became better known as Lawrence of Arabia.

Thomas Edward Lawrence was born in 1885 in North Wales. He studied archaeology at Oxford and took part in digs in the Middle East, where he first came into contact with the Arabs.

He became fascinated by their history and learned their language and culture. This led to him acting as a liaison between the Arab leaders and General Allenby, the British commander of the region during the war.

Lawrence was close friends with Feisal, the son of the Arab ruler, Hussein, and helped organize attacks on Turkish outposts. He became a popular figure among the Arabs and promised them the chance of independence after the war.

Lawrence's force of just 3,000 Bedouin Arabs tied down 50,000 Turkish troops. This figure rose to 150,000 when the uprising grew.

Unfortunately the British turned their back on the Arab cause following the war but Lawrence did not. He argued the case for Arab independence in post-war conferences, feeling the British had not only betrayed the Arabs but had also betrayed Lawrence himself.

Almost as soon as the weather improved in 1918, the Germans started the Spring Offensive...The German commander, Ludendorff, decided to attack near the Somme.

BOOM!

BOOM!

He believed that if he could defeat the British, the French would collapse.

Neighbors are a little noisy today.

Chris, can you nip across and ask them to keep it down?

How can you joke about this? They've been shelling us for days...

The bombardments were always toughest on the newest recruits – and that year we got a lot of new recruits. They all looked like little kids to me.

Did you hear something?

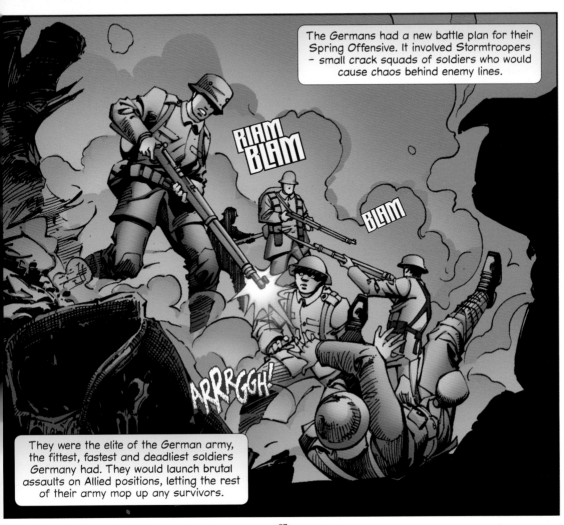

The Germans had a new battle plan for their Spring Offensive. It involved Stormtroopers – small crack squads of soldiers who would cause chaos behind enemy lines.

BLAM BLAM

BLAM

ARRRGGH!

They were the elite of the German army, the fittest, fastest and deadliest soldiers Germany had. They would launch brutal assaults on Allied positions, letting the rest of their army mop up any survivors.

A German shell saved my life. It blew the stormtrooper to kingdom come and would've got me too if I hadn't been flat on my back.

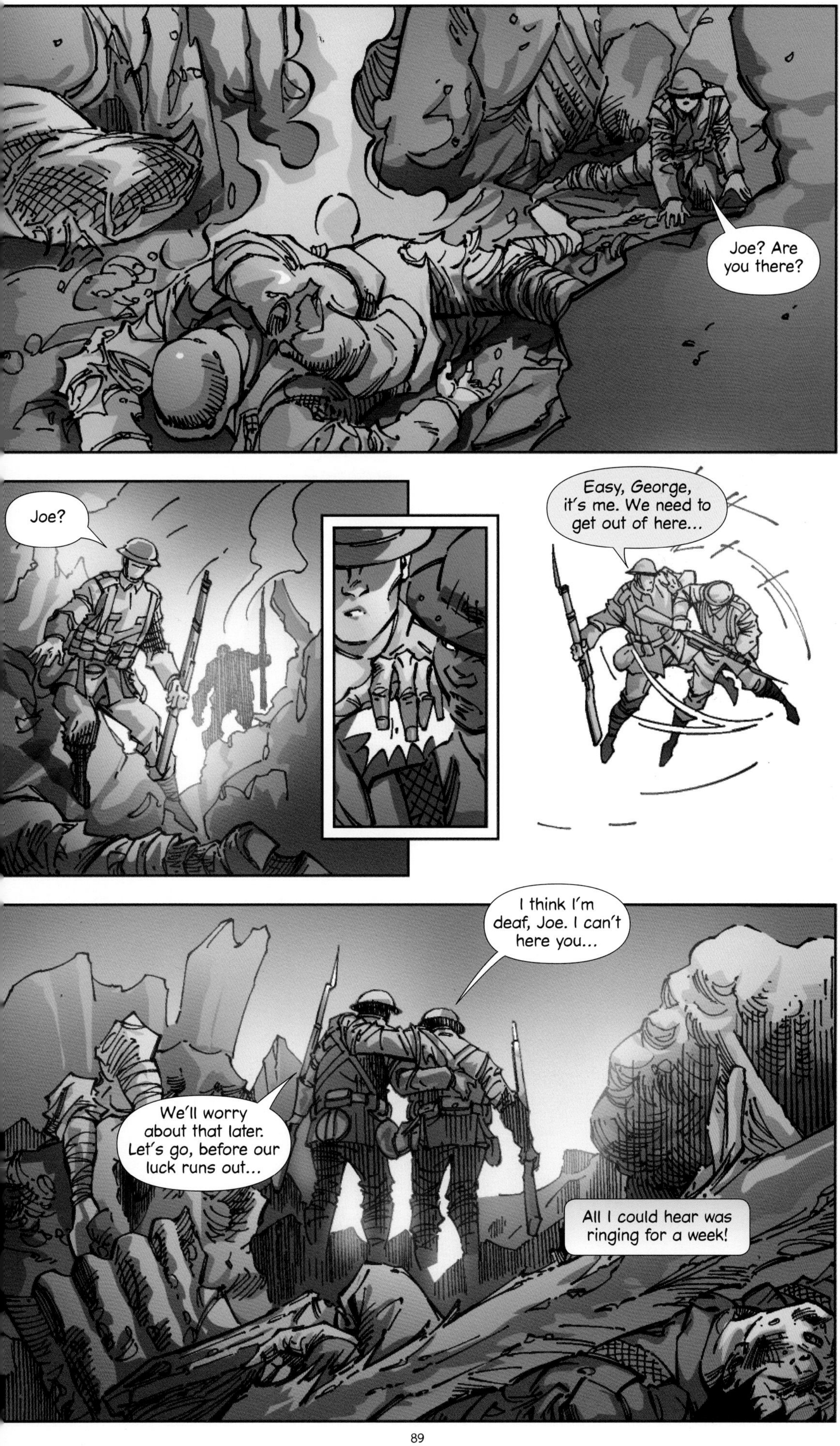

Joe? Are you there?
Joe?
Easy, George, it's me. We need to get out of here...
I think I'm deaf, Joe. I can't here you...
We'll worry about that later. Let's go, before our luck runs out...
All I could hear was ringing for a week!

I met some Germans long after the war. One, Klaus Schmidt, became a good friend. He told me his side of the story and how bad those last months were for him and his friends.

Max, be careful.

I'm too tired to be careful – and too hungry!

Klaus, look at this! Look at all this food!!

Why so sad, at least we can eat now.

They could afford to leave all this food. We haven't eaten for a week. Our supplies are failing... I fear we are losing the war...

Rubbish. Our soldiers are the best in the world. Nothing can stop us.

What we didn't know was just how desperate the situation was for Germany back home. The Allied blockade of their ports was hitting hard, with food shortages taking place across the country.

The German High Command became concerned that riots and unrest back home would spread. If the war was not won soon, their entire way of life would be lost.

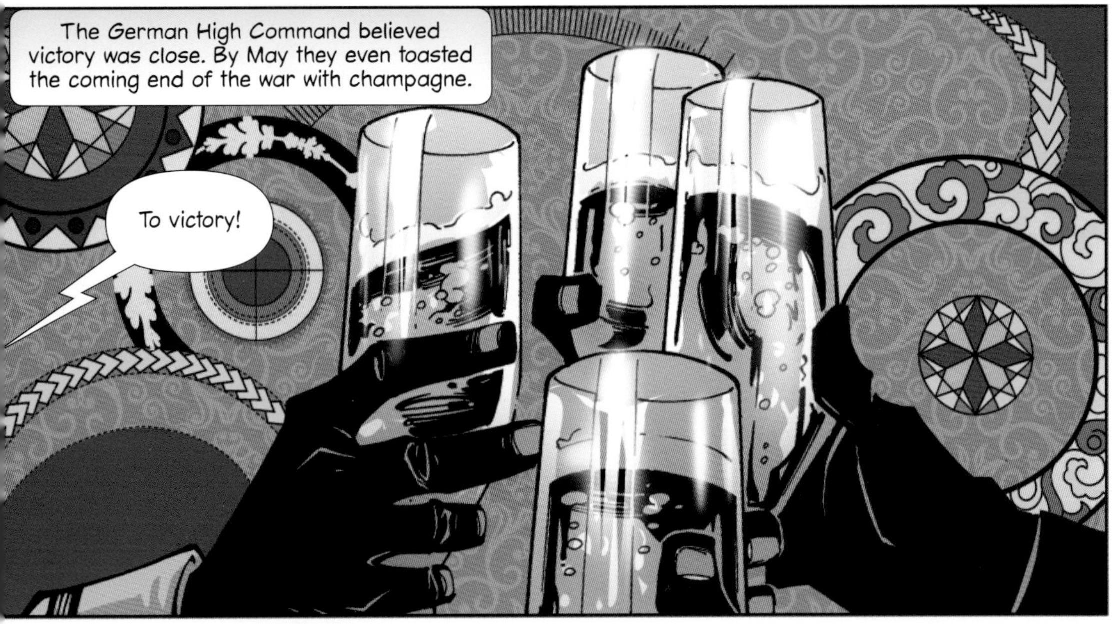
The German High Command believed victory was close. By May they even toasted the coming end of the war with champagne.
To victory!

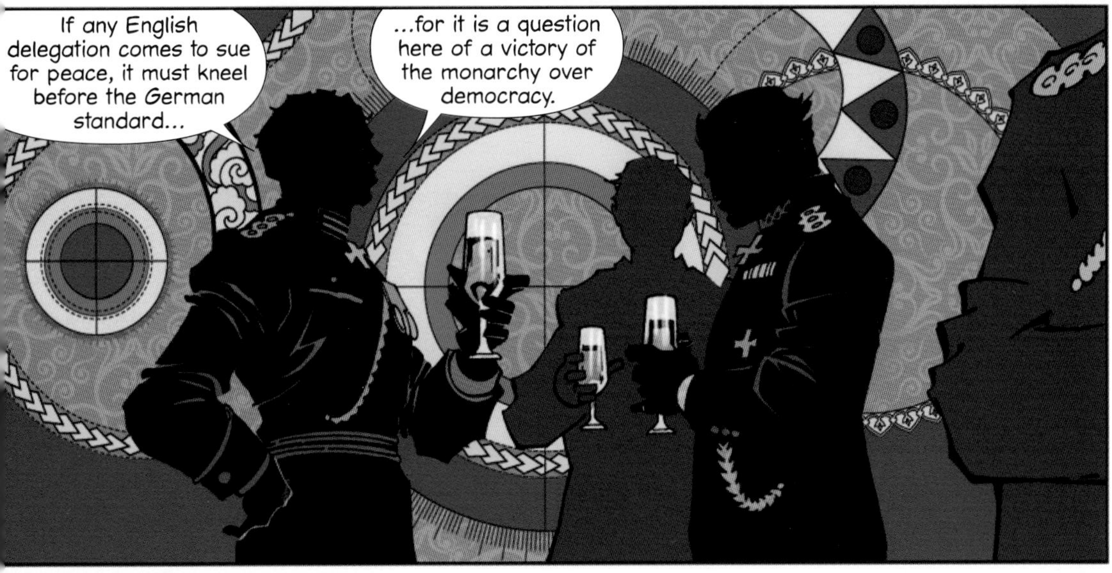
If any English delegation comes to sue for peace, it must kneel before the German standard...
...for it is a question here of a victory of the monarchy over democracy.

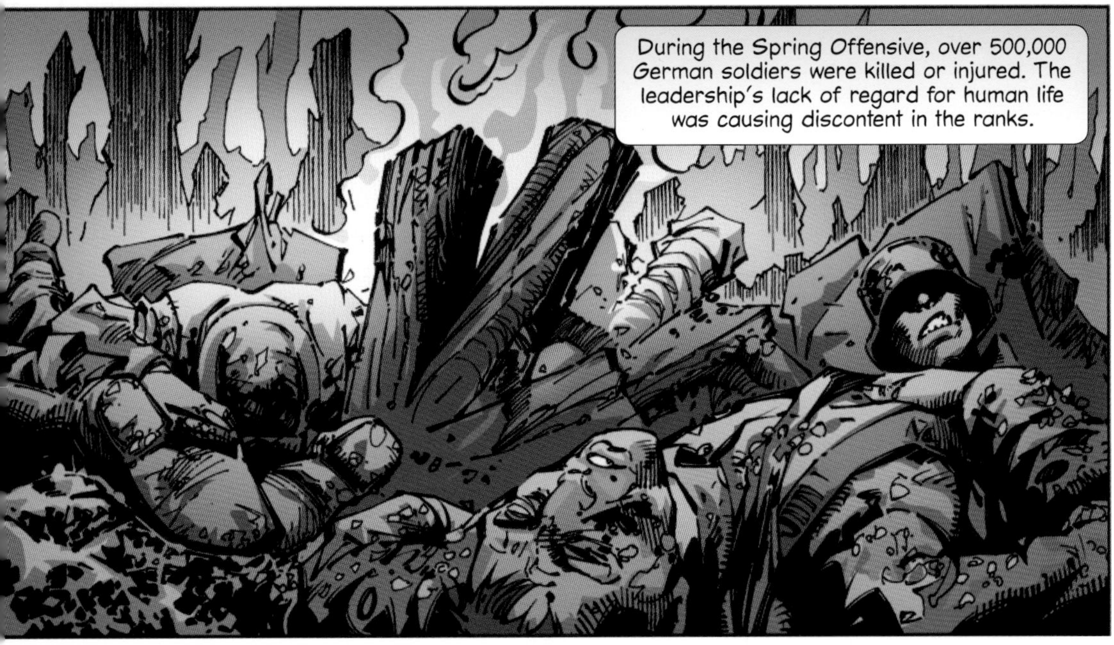
During the Spring Offensive, over 500,000 German soldiers were killed or injured. The leadership's lack of regard for human life was causing discontent in the ranks.

While we advanced, Davy heard from an old friend.

Who's it from?

One of my old pals in the Royal Flying Corps.

"Great bloke called Indra Lal Roy. He loves flying more than anyone I've ever met."

"He's good too. I heard he got ten kills in thirteen days earlier this year."

"A lot of the best pilots are buying it now - on both sides. The Red Baron was killed last week. I know he was a German but he was an amazing pilot."

"His real name was Manfred Albrecht Freiherr Von Richthoffen. They reckon he shot down eighty aircraft between September 1916 and April 1918."

"The Americans have their aces too. Eddie Rickenbacker's good. He was a race car driver before the war and has twenty-six kills to his name. Amazing as he only started last year."

I was hoping to get back up in the air before the end of the war. Reckon there won't be time now.

By March 28th, the Allies were worried. It seemed nothing could stop the German offensive. A meeting of the High Command was called...

The Allied leaders met at Doullens City Hall that day...

The Germans will defeat the English in open country, after which they'll defeat us.

Paris will fall.

Paris has nothing to do with it! Paris is a long way off!

It is where we stand now that the enemy will be stopped.

So what would you have us do?

Oh my plan is not complicated. I would fight without a break.

I would fight all the time and by force of hitting, I would finish by shaking up the Bosche. He's neither cleverer or stronger than we are...

For the moment, it is as in 1914 on the Marne. We must dig in and die where we stand, if need be...

Foch impressed the other leaders so much, he was tasked to coordinate the Allied armies.

Well played, you have the command you wanted.

It is a fine present you've made me. You give me a lost battle and tell me to win it!

93

My hearing wasn't as bad as I'd feared and I was allowed to rejoin the troops a few weeks later.

Things were looking bad though. We'd been retreating constantly.

Gather around men. I have a communiqué to read out from Field Marshal Haig.

Three weeks ago today the enemy began his terrific attacks against us on a fifty-mile front. His objects are to separate us from the French, to take the Channel Ports and destroy the British Army.

"Many amongst us are now tired. To those I would say that victory will belong to the side that holds out longest. The French Army is moving rapidly and in great force to our support."

"There is no other course of action open to us but to fight it out."

"Every position must be held to the last man; there must be no retirement. With our backs to the wall and believing in the justice of our cause each one of us must fight on to the end."

I know it's grim, Joe but come on, don't look so shocked.

What? Oh, sorry. Just had a letter from the wife...

Apparently I've gone and become a dad. Clara's just had a baby...

Did I miss anything important?

Away from the front, and knowing there was trouble ahead, we spent the night celebrating the only good news we'd had in a long time...

Talbot House in Ypres was one of the few places I could relax in. It had a small church in the attic while downstairs was done up like a British home.

To the baby... that's a point. Has it got a name?

Clara wants to call him Fred.

That's a good name...

Hey, what are you guys celebrating?

I've just become a father!

Well, congratulations! We'll have to make sure you get home soon.

You just arrived?

Gosh no, we've been over for months. Just seen my first action at Cantigny.

I was starting to wonder if they'd ever let us see some action!

After all, we'd travelled a long way to be here.

I'm a patriot, right? I love America and all it stands for. So when I heard these Germans wanted to help the Mexicans invade my country, well I went and signed up as soon as I could!

It's not just me either. Germans aren't too popular back home right now. They've stopped teaching the language in schools, got rid of German books from the libraries and even renamed Frankfurters 'liberty sausage!'

You limeys did okay by us though. Let us use your ships to get over here. Some of the boys weren't used to sea travel though and between the overcrowded ship and the constant worry of U-Boat attack, well let's just say it got messy...

After months of training, General Pershing reckoned we were ready for action. I was actually looking forward to it. How dumb is that?

So we took on the Germans at Cantigny for four days from May 28th.

Not sure what the point of the battle was beyond getting the troops blooded, and it did that let me tell you. Now the Germans know they can't mess with Uncle Sam.

Lost some good friends there though. But I guess you guys know all about that...

Welcome to the war...

Over 300,000 US soldiers a month were arriving. And at this stage in the war we were glad to see them.

We needed help, desperately. We were tired and worn out. It didn't help when we heard about the Paris Gun, the Germans' latest super weapon.

They'd unleashed it on March 23rd. It was a massive gun that had to be transported by train and could fire shells over 80 miles — which meant Paris was well within it's reach.

It fired 367 shells at Paris, resulting in 880 casualties — including 250 dead.

As the German offensive continued, we started to retreat further back. All the ground we'd fought so hard to take in the last few years was lost.

We even passed through Passchendaele and I couldn't help thinking about poor old Alex, and what a worthless waste of life it all was.

We did as Haig had asked though and fought for every inch of ground.

We even created Sacrificial Units who would stay behind and allow the others to retreat.

Just before they were overrun, the last soldiers would smash their equipment so it didn't fall into enemy hands...

Then they'd try to make it back to safety...

On July 15th, the Germans launched a fresh assault on the Allies. Twenty-five divisions attacked the French east of Reims and seventeen to the west. It was the *Second Battle of the Marne.*

The *German* attack failed and three days later, Foch arranged a counter-strike. French, Americans, British and Italian forces fought together for the first time.

It was a massive Allied success. Casualties on all sides were high – 95,000 French, 13,000 British and 12,000 Americans – but the *Germans* lost 168,000 and lacked the manpower to replace them.

As the German Chancellor Georg Von Hertling said later, "On the 18th even the most optimistic among us knew that all was lost. The history of the world was played out in three days."

Not only had the tide turned but the Allies had also learned from years of costly mistakes.

All the various elements of the army were now starting to work together. Planes mapped enemy positions so the big guns could bombard them with more accuracy.

While new, improved tanks worked in unison with the foot soldiers, spearheading ferocious assaults.

For the Allied push on Amiens, secrecy was vital. Equipment was moved under cover of darkness...

The Allies now had better equipment – and far more than the enemy.

Each battalion had 30 Lewis guns (portable machine guns). Haig gathered a force of 1,236 field guns and 677 heavy guns for the assault. The Germans had only 530 guns.

The first the Germans knew of the attack was as we advanced at 4.20 AM on August 8th...

Shocked by the speed of our attack, the Germans surrendered *en masse*.

Move along now, move along.

Keep quiet there, Fritz!

Over the course of the day, the Allies advanced up to eight miles and took about 12,000 prisoners.

August 8th was a black day for the German army. Ludendorff offered the Kaiser his resignation but it was refused.

It was now the Germans' turn to retreat.

The scale of the Allied success unhinged Ludendorff, who suffered a nervous collapse. He recovered enough to attend a meeting of the General Staff...

The German army is finished. The war can no longer be won; rather the final defeat is inescapably at hand.

Our only hope is to request an armistice without any hesitation.

When the Allies broke through the Hindenburg line, Germany's defeat became a matter of when instead of if...

On October 30th, the Ottoman Empire in Turkey surrendered, followed quickly by Austria-Hungary on November 3rd.

The Germans tried to make one new defensive line along the Sambre Oise Canal but when the Allies attacked on November 4th, their defense collapsed.

One of my favorite poets, Wilfred Owen, was killed during the fighting, which was the last major battle of the war.

The Germans knew it was over. On the morning of Thursday, November 7th, several cars appeared out of the mist, all bearing white flags. The Germans wanted to negotiate an armistice.

Talks to arrange an armistice took place in Foch's private train.

The agreement was signed at 5.10 in the morning of November 11th with the war set to stop at 11.00 AM.

News went out by wire and quickly spread across the whole world.

The streets of London erupted into one big party!

Everywhere, people cried and laughed at the thought of peace.

It's over. It's finally over. Joe's coming home...

Only the killing didn't stop until the bells rang eleven...

Some officers on both sides refused to send their men out to fight in those last few hours of war...

Others continued to fight until the very last minute.

Canadian soldiers recaptured Mons on the morning of November 11th and some Allied soldiers helped them patrol the outskirts...

Joe, Davy and myself were there. Ironic, as Joe had started the war there four long years before.

As eleven drew closer we started to relax. Peace was coming. We'd made it. We'd survived the war...

The shot came out of nowhere. A sniper chancing his luck one last time.

863 soldiers died on the last day.

My brother Joseph was one of them.

Joe!

George! Get under cover!

Got him. Now for one of his friends...

No, Max. No more killing.

The war is over. Let them live.

There has been more than enough killing...

I was lost. To have come so far...

It just wasn't fair.

I didn't even hear the clock strike eleven.

All I could hear was that final gunshot.

The eleventh hour of the eleventh day of the eleventh month. The war was over. I had survived.

The total cost of the war?
The Allies: 5,520,000 dead; 12,831,000 wounded; 4,121,000 missing.
The Central Powers: 3,386,000 dead; 8,388,000 wounded; 3,629,000 missing.

The war saw the collapse of Imperial dynasties – the Habsburgs of Austria-Hungary; the Hohenzollerns of Germany; the Romanovs of Russia and the Sultans of the Ottoman Empire.

It created a period of vast social, moral and economic change and the world would never be the same again.

They called it the war to end all wars... If only that had been so.

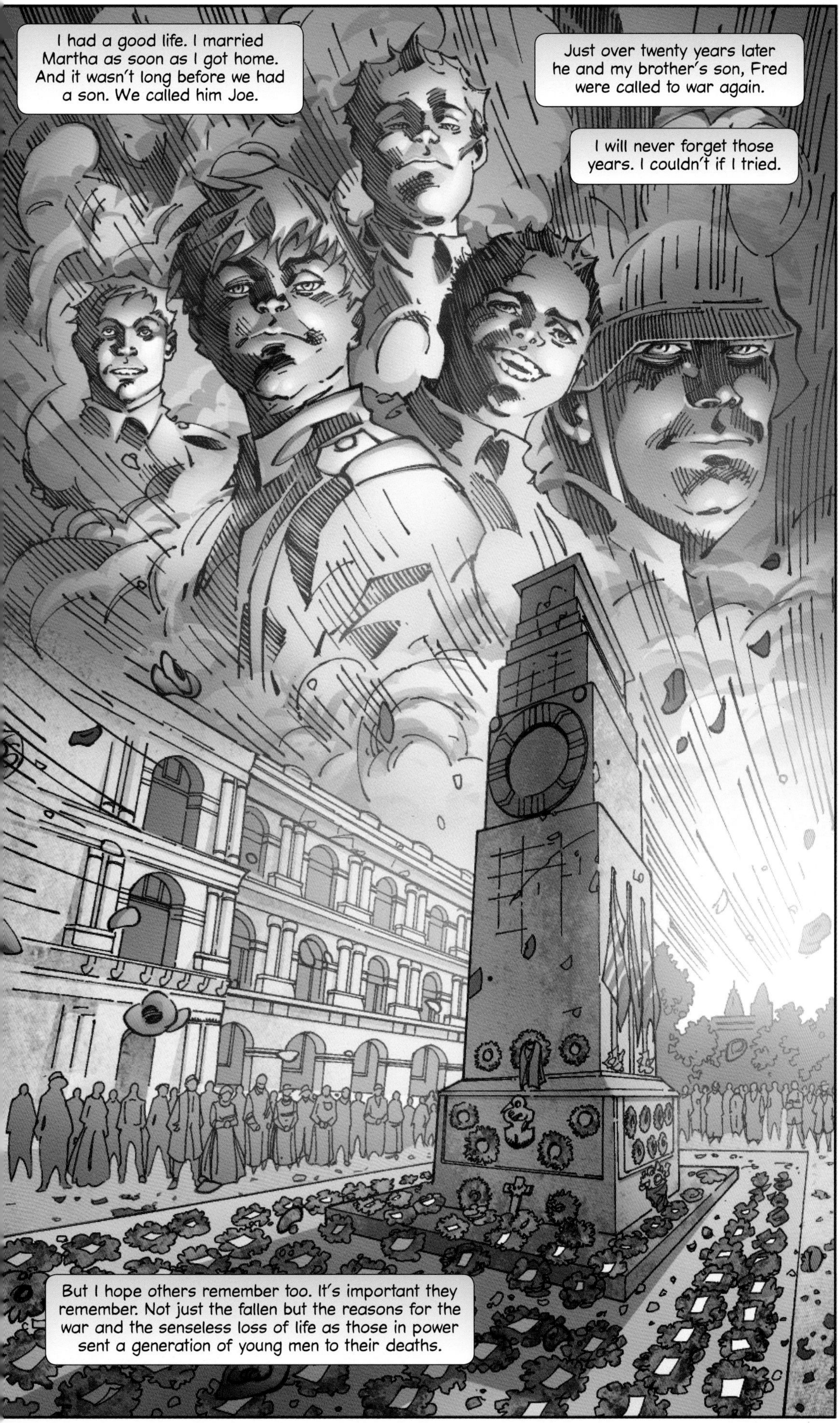
I had a good life. I married Martha as soon as I got home. And it wasn't long before we had a son. We called him Joe.
Just over twenty years later he and my brother's son, Fred were called to war again.
I will never forget those years. I couldn't if I tried.
But I hope others remember too. It's important they remember. Not just the fallen but the reasons for the war and the senseless loss of life as those in power sent a generation of young men to their deaths.

Fred Cowsill, Peter Almond, and Davy Fletcher were real people. Peter survived a gas attack in the trenches and Davy did get expelled from the Royal Flying Corps and sent to the front after hitting an officer. Fred Cowsill died at the Battle of Hooges, July 31st, 1915. This book is dedicated to their memory and to the countless men on all sides who sacrificed their lives and youth.

The red poppy was one of the few plants to grow upon the barren battlefields of World War One. It has now become a symbol of remembrance.

About the Author

Alan Cowsill started out as a comic dealer before becoming a writer and editor. He co-created *Stormwatcher* for Acme/Eclipse before working on Panini UK's Marvel line, writing the first UK-originated *Spider-Man* strips for over a decade. He created the best-selling *Jackie Chan Adventures* and the award-winning *Classic Marvel Figurine Collection* and *DC Super Hero Collection* for Eaglemoss Publishing. He is also one of the key writers and brains behind the Marvel Comics Mini-Series: *Revolutionary War*.

His books include *Colin the Goblin* (Egmont Books), *Warzone: Dark Eden* (Target Games), *Chronopia, DC Comics: A Year by Year Visual Chronicle, Marvel Avengers Character Encyclopaedia, Avengers: The Ultimate Guide To Earth's Mightiest Heroes* and *Spider-Man Year by Year: A Visual Chronicle*. Alan lives and works in London.

About the Artist

Lalit Kumar Sharma was born in Delhi. An artist by nature, he expresses himself through the medium of comic book art. His career as an artist began at Diamond Comics, and since then he has also worked for Raj Comics and all the leading Indian comic book publishers. Dark, grim and dynamic drawing has always been his strong point. At Campfire he has used his strong, action-packed drawing style to illustrate the classics, biographies, and to bring history to life. Lalit lives in his head, and works out of Delhi.

WAS IT REALLY A WORLD WAR?

When we think of World War One we always think of the trenches in France or the Eastern Front in Russia, but what about the rest of the world? As you can see from the map only a handful of nations did not participate in the war, remaining neutral from start to finish.

KEY:
- The Allies
- Central Powers
- Neutral

ASIA AND THE PACIFIC

Japan entered the war at the request of the British in 1914 and they used their fleet to attack German shipping in the Pacific and also took control of many of Germany's island colonies. Japan's interest and influence in China also grew during the war years. By 1915 the Germans had lost all of their territories in the Pacific except for a few small holdouts in New Guinea.

THE INDIAN ARMY

The Indian Army fought not only in France but also at Gallipoli, the Middle East and in East Africa against the German colonial forces. In 1914 the Indian Army was the largest volunteer army in the world, comprising of 240,000 men, by 1918 there were over 548,000. By the end of the war, 90,000 soldiers in the Indian Army had lost their lives.

SOUTH AMERICA

Although several naval battles were fought in the waters around South America, Brazil was the only South American country to become actively involved in the war. Brazil wanted to remain neutral but after several of their merchant ships were sunk by German submarines they eventually declared war in 1917. Brazil's main contribution was naval although they did send a small military mission to Europe to fight amongst their allies.

THE COST IN LIVES

World War One was one of the worst bloodbaths in the history of the planet, claiming over 16,000,000 lives and leaving a further 20,000,000 wounded and maimed. Over 2,000,000 German soldiers were killed in battle and a further 1,000,000 Austria-Hungarian soldiers were also killed. On the allied side, the Russians suffered the greatest number of casualties with over 1,700,000 of their military personnel killed in battle. On the Allied side the French lost 1,400,000 men, the British 900,000 and the US lost over 116,000 men. 65,000 Canadian servicemen lost their lives in the conflict. The Australian and New Zealand Army Corps fought bravely at Gallipoli, France, and the Middle East. In total over 80,000 Australian and New Zealand soldiers lost their lives in World War One.

THE MIDDLE EAST

The Middle East was the scene for some very heavy fighting from October 1914 right up to October 1918. In 1917, the Egyptian Expeditionary Force, made up of British, Indian, Australian and New Zealand troops managed to capture Jerusalem from the Ottoman Empire. Almost a quarter of the entire population of the Ottoman Empire lost their lives during World War I.

SILENT SOLDIERS

The honors heaped upon some of these heroes left them literally speechless; not because they felt humbled but because they were all animals. Let's take a look at some of the strangest animal stories to come out of World War One!

STOP THAT PIGEON!

A homing pigeon called *Cher Ami* managed to save almost 200 American soldiers despite being badly wounded. One day she returned to her loft, shot through the breast, blinded in one eye and with one leg hanging on by just a tendon. Wrapped around that leg was a message from the 'Lost Battalion' of the US 77th Infantry Division. These men had become cut off from the rest of the US Army and were suffering heavy losses. Within hours of receiving the message help arrived and 194 survivors were led away to safety. Surgeons battled fiercely to save *Cher Ami's* life and she was even given a small wooden leg. As soon as she was well enough to travel *Cher Ami* was returned to the United States. The French awarded her with the *Croix de Guerre* medal for heroism.

A FUTURE MOVIE STAR!

When US forces entered the French village of Flirey in 1918, one young corporal rescued a family of puppies and their mother from a bombed out kennel that had been used by the German Army to house their German Shepherd dogs. The corporal took the dogs back to base and after finding homes for the animals he kept one little puppy for himself. He called the dog *Rin Tin Tin*. When he returned to the US after the war, the dog became a massive star of the silent movies. He ended up making 27 movies during his career and was one of the most popular movie stars in the world. Rumor has it that at the first ever Oscars ceremony in 1929, *Rin Tin Tin* received more votes for Best Actor than anyone else, but the Academy decided the award had to go to a human.

SATAN OF VERDUN

Satan was a French messenger dog who helped to save a garrison of French soldiers from destruction during the siege of Verdun. The men were exhausted after being pounded constantly by German artillery. Suddenly they spotted a strange shape running towards them. As it grew closer they realised it was one of their own messenger dogs, *Satan*. He was wearing a gasmask and carrying two baskets on each side of his body. As he drew close he was shot, but he kept moving until he was shot again and again. His trainer ran out to tell his dog to be brave and *Satan* kept moving until he collapsed in his owner's arms. He was carrying a message from the French Army telling them to hold out for a few hours more until reinforcements could arrive. In the baskets were two homing pigeons. The garrison sent a message asking the French to attack the German artillery positions that were bombarding the town and giving the positions of the enemy. One of the birds was shot down but the other got away and within a short time, the French army pinpointed the German battery and silenced it forever.

SERGEANT STUBBY!

An American mongrel called *Stubby* was decorated 11 times during his time of service in World War One. He could salute officers and also warn the men of oncoming gas attacks because his sensitive nose could smell the gas long before it arrived. He took part in 17 battles, managed to track down wounded men in no man's land and he even managed to catch a German spy!

"Keep the home fires burning,
While your hearts are yearning.
Though your lads are far away
They dream of home.
There's a silver lining
Through the dark clouds shining,
Turn the dark cloud inside out
'Til the boys come home."

lyrics by Lena Guilbert Ford
music by Ivor Novello 1914